Life Lessons From Beyond

Life Lessons From Beyond

David C. Hoyt

authorHOUSE®

AuthorHouse™
1663 Liberty Drive
Bloomington, IN 47403
www.authorhouse.com
Phone: 1-800-839-8640

First published by AuthorHouse   10/17/2011

ISBN: 978-1-4634-1457-3 (sc)
ISBN: 978-1-4634-1456-6 (hc)
ISBN: 978-1-4634-1458-0 (ebk)

Library of Congress Control Number: 2011910517

Printed in the United States of America

Contents

Acknowledgments

My sincerest thank you goes to Sue, my wife, my love, and best friend. To our children; Tom and his wife, Carol; Krista and her husband, Greg; and Kyle for being such outstanding citizens.

To our beautiful and talented grandchildren: Taylor, Katelyn, Luke, Bryn, and Ryan. To all of my extended family, past and present, and to all of my friends who have meant so much to me.

A special thank you goes to Krista Evans, who for the book shared her knowledge, wisdom and insights and who is the greatest daughter in the world!

A thank you goes to my editor, Jan Chait, from whom I learned a great deal about writing while working with her. Jan's wit kept me laughing through the process.

Finally, I appreciate greatly the words of Abraham Lincoln when he said, "I have found that folks who have no vices have very few virtues." I continue to take comfort in those words.

Preface

Interestingly, I did not intentionally set out to write this book. I have had very detailed dreams all of my life. Many of my dreams take the form of a short story, an essay, or a full-length feature movie with a plot, sub-plots, and twists and turns to the very end.

That was the case with the dream that became this book. This is the first time I decided to write down what I dreamed. Some chapters are almost word-for-word from the dream. So why did I commit this dream to paper?

I had the dream the night before Krista, our daughter, was scheduled to enter the hospital for the planned delivery of our youngest grandson, Ryan Gregory. Krista lives in Arkansas—three states away from us. The day before the scheduled delivery, my wife, Sue, along with Krista's mother-in-law, Kathy, drove together to be with Krista and her family to provide some help with the children.

The day of the delivery took a traumatic turn. Complications arose during labor that were life-threatening to both Krista and her baby. Ryan was born by an emergency cesarean delivery and immediately had to be resuscitated. Krista received multiple blood transfusions and was taken to the Intensive Care Unit. Sue called me that Monday evening to tell me what Krista and Ryan were experiencing.

Immediately, I left for Arkansas to be with Krista. I needed a distraction from what I was feeling about Krista's emergency. The dream was fresh in my mind, so I began putting ink to paper. It became an interesting experience. The words poured out and filled the pages with what you are about to read. If Krista had a normal delivery, this book would have vanished from my memory as have all of my many previous dreams. A thank you goes to Krista if you enjoy the read. I know it can benefit you.

Thankfully, by the way, both Krista and Ryan are fine. Yes, I do believe in miracles; they have happened to our family.

Also, this book will introduce you to the concept of residual income. Residual income is income for which you are paid multiple times for work done once. Most wealth is created through some kind of residual income. Although the wealthiest among us have utilized residual income to build their wealth, most Americans have not participated to any significant extent. With our changing economy, as technology continues to replace workers, a new paradigm is emerging. Families are seeking multiple streams of revenue, and technology is helping families accomplish that goal.

Finally, the principles are true; the dream I had is true. I believe this book was inspired and was meant to be written and shared with you. There are no coincidences in life; just experiences from which to learn and for which to be grateful. I believe this book will create in you a newfound passion to dream big and make those dreams come true in your life. No doubt!

Introduction

It was nearly ten years ago. I can still see my broken, mangled body lying on the cold, wet cement, blood oozing from my multiple wounds. I was in such pain that I escaped my mortal habitation and hovered above the carnage and the twisted steel. I was at the precipice of a journey that would shatter everything I believed—everything I was taught.

But that experience wasn't the worst day of my life. About two years previous to my near-death experience, or about twelve years ago, my wife, Marilyn—my only true love—was struck and killed by a drunk driver. Instantly, the most beautiful person I ever knew was gone and my life was changed forever.

But the devastation of losing Marilyn and then, almost losing my life is the easiest part of my story to tell—perhaps the only part believable. Sharing all of what happened . . . well, I am not sure that is possible. Yet that is precisely what I'm about to be asked to do.

"Paul. Paul!" My assistant Debbie called, interrupting my reverie.

"Yes Debbie. Sorry, what is it?" I asked, bringing myself back to the present.

"Paul, the reporter has arrived. Shall I show her in?"

"Sure."

Prior to my near-death experience, no one would have wanted to interview me except maybe to report on the homeless. Living in vacant buildings, homeless shelters, and under bridges, life was not what I had dreamed. But that is what my life had become.

Now, this reporter wants me to tell her how all of this happened. How does a person go from hopeless, homeless, and in the depths of despair to joyful, happy, and wealthy beyond what one ever dreams? At that lowest point of my life, I had no education, no special talent, and no resources.

Will she believe me? Will she think I'm as loony as the birds whose sounds pierce the night air here in Montana? Had it not happened to me, I wouldn't believe it. It would be so much easier to explain that I had hit the Powerball Ticket for $30 million.

Debbie shows our guest into my office. "Mr. Fisher, this is Samantha Hodges from New York City representing 'The Life Styles of the Rich Magazine.'"

Samantha is an attractive woman. Just from the manner in which she entered the room and extended her hand, she strikes me as a no-nonsense, fast-paced, career woman with little time to spare. She is nearly my height—and I am 6 feet tall—and is a brunette with a lean and athletic build.

"Hi, Miss Hodges. Is it Miss Hodges?"

"How do you do, Mr. Fisher? Yes, it is 'Miss,' but call me Sam. Everyone calls me Sam."

"Okay, Sam. Please, call me Paul. Thank you, Debbie."

Debbie has been my assistant for the five years I have been in Montana, and I would not know what to do without her. She often brings her children to work with her, and it works out well for everyone.

"It's nice to meet you, Sam. Sit here on the couch and relax. Soft drink, coffee, water, or would you like to try my favorite energy drink?"

"Thank you, water's fine."

"How was your trip here?"

"The first two flights were comfortable. I was a little nervous during the third. I'm not used to flying on such a small plane; but as you know, you are out here in the middle of nowhere, so there wasn't a choice."

"This is heaven on earth, isn't it? That was Crystal Lake you passed about ten miles back. It's fed from mountain streams, but I call the main stream that feeds it Conns Creek. Just reminds me of a creek I used to fish as a kid. It was called Conns Creek. Anyway, didn't that scene of what looks like the lake falling from the mountains make you want to stop and enjoy what Mother Nature provides us?"

"It was beautiful."

"Sam, I never thought I would live in such a place as this. I thought this was only for those special folks you see on TV or in a magazine like yours. Certainly not for me, but here we sit."

"Paul, as I mentioned to you on the phone, we saw the local story published about you when it went over the wire services. Buying land and then giving it away to homeless people will attract a little attention. We did some research and we discovered that just a few years ago, you would have more likely been one of those persons who needed the handout. That's why I am here to learn all of the details of your 'Horatio Alger' or rags-to-riches story, if you will."

"Ah, the details. It's the little foxes that destroy the vine, you know.[1] So, how does this work? How much time do you want to spend together? Obviously we have very little time remaining today."

"The foxes?"

"Never mind."

"Candidly, my editor is not sure to what extent your story has interest to our readers. But, your home is beautiful, and you have what many want today."

"And what is that?"

"The ability to work from your home, to live where you want and to live life on your own terms. I think that's the American dream, don't you? That's a pretty good story. Vince, that's my editor, wanted me to interview you over the phone and have you email us some photographs of your home. I wanted to see Montana and convinced him that your story would be worth my travel expense. So here I am."

"And when are you heading back to the big city?"

"I can get on standby tomorrow if we are finished, but I have my flights arranged for the day after tomorrow. So, I am thinking today, if I just started with a few basic questions, then maybe you could just elaborate and take it from there. You know, rags-to-riches, how you did it, why you give land to the homeless, that kind of thing. Just get started. Then tomorrow we could wind it up, and I could take some photographs of your home and property. I don't want to take too much of your time."

Sam has no idea how interested her readers would be if I were to tell her the entire story. I won't. I can't. What happened to me is so unbelievable, so bizarre, and so paranormal, I can't tell her. I feel very akin to those people who believe they saw a UFO or Big Foot and chose to keep it to themselves because they didn't want the publicity or the ridicule.

Here's what's hard to understand. What happened to me is true; I have the evidence of its truth. Yet, I question that evidence even today. How can that be? I'm still wondering that myself. That's why I have only shared this with one person. One thing I know is that we are not alone, and we are not the most intelligent creatures of this universe. I know that.

"So tell me Paul; where did it all begin for you?"

Chapter 1

The credit belongs to the man who is actually in the arena;
Whose face is marred by dust and sweat and blood;
Who strives valiantly; who errs and comes up short again and again;
Who knows the great enthusiasms, the great devotions,
And spends himself in a worthy cause;
Who at the best knows in the end the triumph of high achievement;
And who at the worst, if he fails, at least fails while daring greatly.
—Theodore Roosevelt, 1858-1919
President of the United States,
Governor of New York;
Decorated war hero, Medal of Honor Recipient,
Hunter, conservationist

"Well Sam, I had a happy childhood. We had a small, one-bedroom home, and we could not afford to take vacations. I went to an inner city school. I certainly didn't know we had very little until I became an adult and began understanding what my parents went through to provide for us.

"I grew up with three older sisters—in that one-bedroom home. I went to college, but wasn't smart or athletic enough to have it all come easily to me. After my first year, I knew college wasn't for me. So I left, went back home, and got a job at our local post office.

"Then I met Marilyn, Marilyn Beal. She was so beautiful, so athletic, and with a smile that would warm the winter air. It was love at first sight for me, maybe not for her. However, I grew on her and we finally began dating. We fell in love. We married and thought we would buy the house with the picket fence, have two or three children, and live happily ever after.

"We rented an apartment while we saved our money for our first home. Scenic View Apartments was the name of where we lived, never will forget that. The first year we were together was the happiest time of my life. Have you ever felt that things were just too good to be true? That's how I felt. I guess for good reason because soon came the worst day of my life."

"What happened?"

"As I was driving home from work on a cold December day, I suddenly felt like I was hit by a truck. I could hear my heart pounding, but I didn't know why. Then, I had this eerie feeling come over me that I would never see Marilyn again. I felt panicked. I sped home, a forty-minute drive that seemed to never end, only to find a police car pulling up to the apartment at about the same time I arrived.

"My deepest fears were about to be realized. The police officer told me that at exactly 3:48 that afternoon, about the same time I had the feeling something was wrong, Marilyn was struck and killed by a drunk driver. The drunk driver was also killed."

"That had to be devastating."

"It changes your world forever. Nothing comforts you. The funeral arrangements, the visits from many family and friends, the funeral itself, all passed as if it were a nightmare from which I could not awaken. I just couldn't even think about going back to work. I lost my job, the apartment, and eventually moved back home with my parents.

"What I didn't know until a month after moving in with my parents was that my father had been fighting cancer for three months. He was not one to share burdens with his family. Mom knew, but neither would tell me because of the grief I was already experiencing. Two months later, he died.

"As if that weren't enough, within a year, my mother was diagnosed with cancer and she, too, died. I guess she just needed to be with him, or maybe he needed her to come up and be with him. I don't know. At this time in my life, I was pretty sure that when you died, there just wasn't much else to it. I felt that my life was crashing down around me."

"What did you do next?"

"Well, the house was worth very little and after the four of us—my three sisters and me—paid for the funeral, medical bills, and a few small debts mother had, the sale of the house barely covered our expenses. I had to leave. The love of my life, Marilyn, dies, my father, and now my mother. I never felt greater despair."

"Where did you go?" Sam asks.

"I still had my car, an old Pontiac Bonneville. So I headed to Cleveland where I had a friend, Mark Shields, from my year in college. Mark worked with his father's company that manufactured body armor and thought I could be successful as a sales representative. After a few months of trying, it just wasn't working out. I was sure I needed to find a job where I had no responsibilities, no interaction with people and, at the end of the day, no worries to take home from work."

"And how did that work out?"

"It worked out okay, it's just that those kinds of jobs generally don't allow you to live the American dream, or so it seemed to me to be the case at that time."

"Are you suggesting that for some, those kinds of jobs are the American dream?"

"No, not exactly. How do I explain it? Let me come back to that later. But I couldn't even hold down those jobs. I got to where I had no hope; I had no ambition, and I felt I had no future. I thought I was a pretty good guy all of my life. I met the girl of my dreams, and I had confidence we could make our place in this world. Where my life had come to now, I felt something must be wrong with me to have allowed this to happen. I just couldn't bounce back. I was a lost soul if ever there was one.

"Then, life changed again forever. It happened while standing on a busy intersection holding a sign that read, 'Will Work for Food.' Of course, believe me, I did not want to work for food. I just wanted your generous donation. Everyone has an opinion of those people standing on the street corner. Now I was one. I was just numb to everyone and everything. I saw none of the possibilities that life holds. I could see only the obstacles, and the obstacles seemed enormous."

"What happened?"

"A lightening bolt from the sky is what happened!

"I am going to get me an energy drink. Can I get you anything, Sam?"

"No, thanks."

Chapter 2

---

*Firmness of purpose is one of the most necessary
Sinews of character, and of the best instruments of success.
Without it, genius wastes its efforts in a maze of inconsistencies.*
—Lord Chesterfield, 1694-1773
British Statesman, Politician, Man of Letters

"So, you were starting to tell me that a life-changing event was about to take place while you were standing on a street corner begging for money."

"Sam, that sounds so harsh when you say it like that. But, yes, that's what I was doing. It was a cold afternoon in Southfield, near Detroit. I picked out my spot in the median nearest to a left-hand turn lane. You get the picture. You want to be where cars have to stop and look at you. Technically, you want the drivers to look at you. Anyway, many get so embarrassed that they finally dig into their pockets for some money."

"Do you believe those who give money are doing it out of embarrassment?"

"Some. Not all. Many sincerely want to help you and feel good to be able to share their good fortune with you. There are those who won't look at you and pretend they don't notice you. Then there are those who think that you're not worthy of help since you chose to be there.

"Believe it or not, some who stand on the corner are more ambitious than others. They have their favorite corners and won't allow anyone to 'move in' on their territory.

"I just wanted enough money to stop at McDonald's for food, get an occasional room at a cheap motel to shower, and remind myself what a bed felt like. Then, I would get on down the road to another city. I traveled and slept in my car until it gave out. I hoofed it afterwards or hitchhiked, then sometimes I slept under bridges or found a cot in a homeless shelter. You are always trying to avoid the notice of a police officer. But, I was picked up for vagrancy a couple of times, and that is where my life had come. Can you imagine that?"

"No, I can't. Get back to your life-changing event on the street corner. What happened?"

"It began as a typical encounter. I saw the window dropping down to expose a hand holding a dollar bill reaching my way. I made my way to the driver and thanked him for his generosity. The last thing I remember was an explosion and being tossed in the air like a rag doll. They measured I'd landed more than one hundred feet from the collision. Like a cruel repeat of what happened to Marilyn, a drunk driver slammed into me and the car that stopped to help me.

"What I learned next was that when your body is so racked with pain you wish you could leave it, you do. Or, at least your spirit leaves. Mine did."

"Paul, are you saying you had, or at least believe you had, an out-of-body experience? I have heard these kinds of tales, but I have never met someone who actually claimed he experienced one."

"Well, you have now. Yes. That's exactly what happened. I could feel my spirit leave my body, and suddenly, the pain was gone. From above the carnage and twisted steel, I watched as the first responders, folks who were just driving by and saw the wreck, came to help. One brought a blanket and covered my body. She must have believed I was still alive as she left my face exposed. Two police cars arrived next, then a rescue truck from the fire department and finally, the ambulance. I watched as they all did their work efficiently and professionally. The driver who caused the crash died. The one who gave me the dollar survived."

"So your wife, Marilyn, a few years earlier was killed by a drunk driver, and now you are battling for your life after being struck, also by a drunk driver? And your spirit is hovering above the accident watching the emergency personnel working on your body? Seriously?"

"Seriously. Ironic, isn't it? It ended up being one of the greatest things to ever happen to me. Don't get me wrong. I'm sure I felt differently at that moment, and I still feel sorrow for the family of the driver who died in the accident. But for me, it was from heaven."

"How so?"

How so? She is definitely not going to believe this one.

5

Chapter 3

All I have seen teaches me to trust the Creator for all that I have not seen.
—Ralph Waldo Emerson, 1803-1882
American author, poet, and philosopher

How can I break this to her? If she wants to know the real reason I have such uncommon joy and success, she's going to have to accept a new paradigm from her reality. Can I share with her my "Seven Secrets for Living Life Abundantly" I learned without telling her where I learned it? That's what I've been doing with those in my business. I mean, this didn't come from any book. But, how do you tell someone with the skeptical nature of a journalist you were in an advanced training session on "how to live life abundantly," while everyone around you believed you were in a coma? And, believe me, that would be the easiest part to share.

"How so? That question, Sam, requires a thoughtful answer and maybe your open mind. But, I'll try to answer it. For a significant period of time, I wasn't confined to my body."

"Help me understand that and frankly, to believe it."

"Remember, I said I was so badly injured I actually left my body and could watch as all of the emergency crew worked on me. I was taught our spirit resides in our body, and our body is simply a transport device to chauffer us around during this existence. Under duress, your spirit sometimes leaves its body to avoid the pain of its mortal existence. During that time, you don't want to return. It's a very joyful experience."

"You were taught this? In Church? Paul, I can remember learning the idea in Church we are made up of body, mind, and spirit and our spirit leaves our body at death to eventually return to heaven, or at least we hope that's where we go. I grew out of such beliefs as I went through school.

I have concluded we have invented God to control the masses. I would never tell my parents that of course. They are Catholic."

It amazes me that our great country was founded on the principles that it was our Creator—not man—who has endowed us with our unalienable rights. But so many young people are leaving higher education with the belief man created the Creator. Sam, most definitely, will have trouble with what I'm about to share.

"Sam, I was taught this, but not in Church. I didn't grow up in a family that went to Church regularly. I know you will have trouble with this one, I assure you; I was taught this by Marilyn."

"Marilyn? So before her passing, she taught you her religious beliefs?"

"No, she taught me from her actual experience. You see, she taught me from the spirit world after her death, and while my body was comatose."

This is my first attempt to test Sam's tolerance for what she may think is from the twilight zone. If she thinks this is crazy, then she certainly won't be ready for the rest of this story. After all, the only person I've shared this story with believed I may have had too many drugs during my time in the hospital. I won't go through that again.

"Your deceased wife who died a few years earlier visited you while you were in a coma? She taught you about the spirit world from the spirit world? Are you serious?"

"It was more like I visited her. Or should I say, I was taken to her while out of my body. I know how this sounds, but here's what happened:

"When the ambulance arrived and took me to the hospital, I, or my spirit, just knew I was going to die. I wanted to. I never felt freer. All of the pain, all of the stress, was gone. I had the freedom to go where I wanted immediately and without restriction. I didn't understand why or how, but heck, I don't understand why or how most things in this life work. Why would I, all of a sudden, know how these very weird things that were suddenly happening to me worked?

"I visited each of my siblings. Oh, they didn't know I was there with them and probably wouldn't have believed that. I watched as they learned of my accident. I wanted to comfort them and tell them how wonderful I felt, but I couldn't. Time meant nothing. If I thought it, I did it."

"Let me understand you. Your spirit was traveling, at what? At the speed of light making visits to your families' homes? Blink your eyes and you were wherever you wanted to be? Is that right?"

"That's what was happening. Then suddenly, I had a companion. More like a messenger. I thought of him a 'The Messenger' because I would never be without him leading me through whatever I was going through. He made me aware I was expected to go with him. I did."

"Go where?"

"It was a very beautiful place. I can't describe it. There aren't words in our language. 'Bright, brilliant, peaceful, joyful, calming' . . . none even begins to describe it accurately. It's bright, but the brightness doesn't hurt your eyes. Instead, you bask in it. The joy and calm are indescribable. You suddenly see the life you lived clearly—every detail, good, bad, and indifferent. You realize the errors of your ways instantly. You see the limits you placed upon yourself you could so easily have lifted.

"You instantly know there is no 'average Joe,' and we were all created to love and be loved, enjoy, prosper, and live life abundantly. Laughter was to be a normal state. That we place such emphases on such things as IQ, looks, athleticism, status, and the right clothes is foolish. All of the things we believe are important, aren't. I was so joyful to be in that moment. Then you have a flood of despair that envelops you."

"Despair?" Sam asks.

"Yes. Your despair is for the life you could have had, but did not live. All of the possibilities are so clear and distinct, and you know you could have had such a complete and full life had you chosen. The obstacles you saw as so great while you were on this planet are but tiny grains of sand that could have been stepped over without a thought."

"Paul, I remember in my world religion course in undergraduate school that the Talmud said 'a person will be called to account on judgment day for every permissible thing he might have enjoyed but did not.' Is that what you thought you were experiencing?"

"I think so. You instantly know everyone is programmed for a life of uncommon joy and abundant living. We are meant to enjoy all we can. It's only a few who don't lose this program through life's experiences. Then, it's even fewer who are able to find it once it's been lost."

"I am sorry, lose what or find what? I think I missed something while taking notes."

"We come into our lives programmed for uncommon success and a life of abundance. Most people lose that 'know-how' and never find it again during their lives. But a few do find it later in their lives, and they're the lucky ones. They're the blessed ones."

"And you learned this while visiting the spirit world as your body was being transported to the hospital after being hit by a drunk driver? Paul, please take no offense, but did you spend time with a psychologist as part of your rehabilitation? I mean, this does sound pretty delusional, don't you think? Whoops, my cell phone is vibrating. I'm sorry, Paul, can you give me a minute?"

Chapter 4

One of the hardest lessons we have to learn in this life,
And one that many persons never learn, is to see the divine,
The celestial, the pure in the common, the near at hand—
To see that heaven lies about us here in this world.
—John Burroughs, 1837-1921
Naturalist, conservationist, essayist

I knew it. She said she's not a believer in life after death. She thinks I'm a space cadet? I've just shared the easy part. If she thinks I'm delusional now, just wait. I have to change the direction of this interview.

Sam returns, "I'm sorry for the interruption. Where were we? Let me see here. Your wife, Marilyn, died. You lost your job, your apartment, your father died, and your mother died. You went off the deep end, lived under bridges and begged for money to buy food. Then, you were hit by a car that killed the driver and almost killed you, and you went to visit your deceased wife in the spirit world while lying comatose in the hospital. Is that about it?"

"Sam, maybe we should cover just exactly how I've done so well these past few years. After all, you wanted a 'rags-to-riches' story, didn't you? You have the rags part of it, so let's get to the riches part, and that should get you the story you want. Does that sound like a plan?"

"Yes, I think that would be fine. Then tomorrow I can take some photographs and be on my way. Don't get me wrong; it is interesting what you've said, but that's not what our magazine is about. Maybe, Paul, your next interview should be with a paranormal magazine." Sam laughed.

"Okay. After eight months of lying in a vegetated state, I opened my eyes. I was a small shadow of my former self, but I was aware of what happened, had a renewed enthusiasm for this life, and couldn't wait to begin anew. It would be more than a month before I was moved from the hospital to a rehabilitation clinic. Although my brain was racing with newfound knowledge and excitement for the possibilities I could now see so clearly, it would be some time to be able to get back to a normal existence. The collision had broken almost every bone from my waist down, half of my ribs, internal injuries too numerous to describe, yet I had a chance to return to good health. I knew positively I would.

"Thanks to great doctors, nurses, the best health care system in the world, and a lot of rehabilitation, I did return to good health. What a blessing! With no insurance, just Medicaid since I had no job or money, I built quite a debt to my fellow taxpayers. But I'm doing my best to pay that back. You know, helping those who need it."

"Paul, how long did it take for you to get back on your feet?"

"It took more than a year after coming out of the coma. Fortunately for me, I had a support team, including my three sisters, their husbands and a very special friend. None would give up on me. I would spend a few weeks with one family and then a few weeks with another. The goal was not to inconvenience any one family for too long. I am so grateful for each of them and will always cherish those times."

"Let me ask you about your business. How did you choose the business you have? How did you get started? With no money, how did you build a business from scratch to what it is today?"

"Good questions. When I wasn't working on my body, learning to walk again, regaining my strength and body weight, I was investigating business opportunities. I knew I wanted to find the correct opportunity for me. I wanted a business I could start up with a minimum amount of capital since I had none, and I wanted an opportunity I had a chance to succeed at. As is often the case, the drunk driver who hit me had no assets and had no insurance so there would be no windfall from his estate. I was ready to do whatever it took to succeed, and I also knew I had all of the tools necessary to succeed. I could only go up.

"I began reading about how to start your own business. I learned that earning a living or starting a business is all about leveraging what you have in exchange for what you want. However, I did not have much to leverage. For example, I learned that there are at least seven kinds of 'assets' you can leverage into income:

1. Your ability to work
2. Your money
3. Other people's money
4. Knowledge
5. Skills
6. A unique system
7. The efforts of other people

"*Work* is what most people do to create income. That's what a job is all about. But the person you're working for is leveraging your efforts into company profits.

"Let's look at '*your money*.' You may be saving and investing your money. That is your money making you money. Many people believe you have to have money to make money; but it's just one of the ways we can make money. I didn't have any money.

"How does one earn money with '*other peoples' money?*' Banks do it. They use money from their customers' checking accounts, low-paying savings accounts, and CDs and lend that money to other customers at a higher interest rate. Here's a simple example. If someone lends you money at three percent and you earn five percent, then you've successfully made money from another person's money. You've acted similarly to a bank.

"*Knowledge* can be leveraged into income. Many fields such as teachers, doctors, and attorneys require an education that can create income. Others will pay for that knowledge. I had one year of college, so I didn't have any special knowledge to leverage into income.

"*Skills* are leveraged into income. A carpenter, an athlete, and an actor are examples of individuals with skills they can leverage into income. I had no marketable skills.

"*Systems* can be leveraged into income and can create great wealth. Ray Kroc, founder of McDonald's, is an example. He developed a system of delivering food people wanted in a faster manner than available. 'Fast food' is a result of that system, and he did pretty well for himself. Sam Walton of Wal-Mart knew he could provide the goods and services people wanted for less money. Wal-Mart is an example of a unique delivery system. Bill Gates used technology as a unique system to create wealth. I had no unique system.

"Businesses leverage *other peoples' efforts*. As I mentioned, the jobs most people have are 'leverage' to the businesses that hired them. Employees are employed in order to provide more profit for the businesses that hire them. So, I'm thinking; what do I have to leverage into income?"

"Paul, where are you learning about these things? Did you spend time in the library, attend workshops, travel the internet? How are you getting this knowledge?"

"I incorporated all of the above, Sam. I would also introduce myself to people who looked successful: ones I saw in restaurants, the church I began attending—anywhere. I had a new thirst for knowledge.

"Then, I came across an article about *residual income*. It explained that residual income acts like passive income. It is income for which you work once, but are paid again and again. For example, an insurance agency is built on residual income. The agent makes the sale once and is paid each time the customer renews his coverage. An actor can be paid each time his movie is shown at the theater or on the TV. A money manager may receive, every year, a percentage of the money he is managing. An author writes a book once and is paid each time someone buys it. I knew I wanted to start a business that could provide residual income!

"The next morning after reading the article about residual income, I was having breakfast in a McDonald's restaurant. I noticed a young woman enthusiastically leading a discussion at a nearby table. I began eavesdropping on her conversation. It became apparent it was more of a presentation.

"She was telling the others about a particular nutrition product she began taking that changed her life. Her energy, focus, and feeling of wellness significantly improved. Joint pain she experienced for years had disappeared. It was a rich vitamin and mineral supplement that had many of the necessary ingredients doctors and nutritionists recommend to their patients.

"She told them the product was being marketed by word of mouth, and said she was a customer. Instead of the company paying millions of dollars for advertising, promotion and stocking the product on the store shelves, the company paid customers to share the story with other potential customers. She told her listeners they'd be surprised to hear how much potential income one can earn doing this business.

"Then I heard her say the magic words: *residual income*. You make the sale once, she said, but people order it month after month because it works for them. Every time they reorder, you get paid again. You are paid on the sales of not only your efforts, but the efforts of many others.

I needed the nutrition, and I was looking for residual income. Here was a business that provided residual income and the leverage of other peoples' efforts. I thought, 'could this be the leverage I was looking for?'

"So after she completed her presentation, I approached her and introduced myself. Her name was Jean Irving. Jean was one of those people who loved what she was doing and was an enthusiastic communicator with good people skills. I asked her about the product and ended up purchasing a month's supply. Although a modest cost, it was about all of the money I had.

"Within a few weeks, I could tell it worked for me and was convinced it would work for others. After that first month, I called Jean to see if there was an opportunity for someone like me without much money to do what she was doing. My rehabilitation was coming to an end, but I was still without money. The family member I was living with was pulling all of the weight for our living expenses and taking care of me. I felt like a lion wanting out of its cage.

"What I learned about her business was that she is paid to do two things simultaneously: She is paid to gather customers by telling people about her product and then to ask them if they would like to make some additional income. So in essence, she has developed a retail business of people using the product and a wholesale distribution business of people doing the same thing. Both were profit centers. I was hooked on the idea.

"Since I was broke, the best part was I did not have to purchase inventory. My customers could go directly to the company and purchase the product, and I got the credit for the purchase. I would learn how to teach others to do the same thing and earn money introducing a great nutrition product to others. The more success they had, the more success I had. Here is a business with no significant capital requirement which leverages other peoples' efforts into income, and the income generated is residual income. I was excited."

"Paul, you said Jean, the person whom you met in the restaurant, had good people skills and was a good presenter in front of a group. What made you think you could do the business she was doing—given all you had been through?"

"Actually, I thought that might be the catch. I didn't have the skills she had, and I didn't think I could teach others about nutrition. I had already proven to myself—at my friend's business in Detroit—I couldn't sell anything. So, I feared maybe this wasn't for me.

"Jean asked me if I could put a DVD in a DVD player. I said I could. She asked me if I could hand out a sample of the product. I said I could. She said that's all you need to do to get started. She said to just find a few people who are open-minded and could also operate their DVD player, and then give them samples of the product. That sounded too easy; but I had nothing to lose, so I gave it a try.

"I became a distributor. I had already purchased some product. I took the company's training program and began my business. Even though I had a company to buy my products from, receive my training, and had the camaraderie of thousands of other distributors, I was a self-employed independent distributor who could build my business anywhere I wanted. So that is just what I did and it worked.

"Today, if my prospect can visit a web site, play a DVD player, or give a person a sample to try, he or she has a chance to be successful at this business. Then, if they follow my strategies for living life abundantly, their success is guaranteed!"

"In all due respect, Paul, no one has great success without extraordinary talent or skill to achieve success. Wouldn't you agree that today you have skills others don't have?"

"I had desire and was willing to take the first steps to get started. Yes, I have skills today I didn't have when I took those first steps. These skills come as you go through the process and given what I learned. For example, when I first started, it took me forever to find the first person who wanted to do this business. Now, the majority of people I introduce the business to join me. So skills and confidence come with success. But I knew I would have the success because of what I learned."

"So, Paul, from scratch, you built this endeavor into a very lucrative business. Again, how do you do that given where you were before the accident, standing on a street corner with a sign that said 'Will Work for Food?' You said you had no ambition."

Here we go again. Really, I know I couldn't have had my success without the newfound knowledge I received while visiting Marilyn in the spirit world. Sam doesn't want to hear or believe that. I guess few people would be open to such a story. It keeps coming back to the same thing; my reality is not going to be accepted which is why I've always wanted to avoid this discussion. I'm thinking; 'let's just give her what she wants to hear and not complicate it.'

"Well Sam, I worked hard, approached my family and friends first, showed them how my product would benefit them, asked them to support me in my new business and showed them how they could do the same: that is, make some extra income while showing others the product. If they followed my success formula, they could buy a new car, take a vacation, or even buy a vacation home—all with the extra income they could earn while keeping their current job. It worked for me and for them. This year, our revenue will approach fifty million dollars!"

"How long did it take?"

"Sam, what I learned was if you work really hard at first, you'll feel like you're working for very little. The results take time. Also, to which you alluded, I had to develop skills. So while I felt I was being underpaid at first, I started getting overly paid later. It took me about a year before it started getting interesting. But when it started getting interesting, it got very interesting, very fast. I'm so thankful I stayed after it. Many quit during the beginning.

"In my third year, I began visiting here in Montana, found a real estate broker, and finally found this property for sale at a price I could actually afford. Two thousand acres and I could afford it. Unbelievable! Then I found an architect and a builder, and we designed this home. Nearly a year later, I moved in, and it has been just great ever since."

"Paul, the homes we feature in our magazine are usually quite ostentatious and often worth upward of ten million dollars. You have a beautiful home, but not of that kind. What unique qualities does it have I can *sell* to my editor, Vince, so we can get this story in the magazine?"

She has a story of a lifetime and doesn't recognize it. Every person not living a life of joy and abundance would die for this information, no pun intended. I almost did. I guess I spent in earth terms, eight months in the spirit world, learning from my deceased wife how to have everything a person wants while living in this life—and that's just the beginning. But Sam isn't ready for any of that, and maybe that's best. I've taught my fellow business associates the success formula without telling them where I learned it. Maybe that's what I'm to do; just teach those who need to learn it and are ready to learn it, so they can have all of what they want.

"Well, Sam, I'm not exactly sure, but let me show you around. You have seen the entry, the family room, and the sitting area. Obviously this is my office and where I spend part of my day. Follow me this way to the patio and pool area. The home is everything I wanted. It was designed to fit into the environment, take advantage of the solar heat, and is referred to as a 'green' structure: that is, it's built environmentally friendly. It's about ten thousand square feet and maybe that's not very big for homes in your magazine, but it's everything I ever dreamed. In fact, it's exactly as I dreamed."

"Paul, the pool is beautiful. It looks like there is no end to it."

We designed it to take advantage of the spectacular view of the mountains and the sunset. With the sunken patio that surrounds the pool, it's perfect for entertaining, and, I believe, provides a spectacular setting."

"You're right. I love the way you have taken advantage of the evening light. It's a stunning view, isn't it?"

"I believe so. Come back inside and let me show you the 'brains' of the place.

"Here's the computer room. It's a smart home. The computer there, I call Lisa. She actually speaks to me every morning. She unlocks the house, uncovers the pool, turns on the lights as I enter a room, and turns them off as I leave. She makes me coffee, brings up my emails, text messages, voice messages, and just makes life pretty easy.

"This hallway takes us to the garage and work area. You can see I enjoy collecting classic Harley-Davidson motorcycles. I had the garage built to accommodate my passion. I like working on them. It's a stress reliever for me."

"You have quite a collection. Do you ride often?"

"As often as I can. I never get tired of riding through these foothills and up into the mountains."

Paul pushes a button to raise the garage door to reveal another scenic view of the property and surroundings. "And nothing I could ever have built can come close to the majesty of the land. That's the real beauty here and why I'm blessed to be here."

"It is beautiful, Paul. Okay. Why don't we call it a day? I will plan to come by tomorrow and take some photographs. Then maybe your assistant, Debbie, can walk me through the rest of the house and drive me around your property. If there is anything else I need for the interview, can I have a minute with you after I take some photos?"

"Of course. You're welcome to stay here if you'd like; we have plenty of room. Maybe not as opulent as you're used to in New York, but comfortable."

"I can't. Company policy. I have a reservation for that little motel a few miles back. I think it was the only place within an hour. It looked about as opulent as I'm used to. Thanks so much for your time, Paul. I've enjoyed it."

"You're welcome. We'll see you tomorrow. By the way, I think you'll be pleasantly surprised by the motel where you're staying.

"Debbie, show Sam the flower garden on her way out. She'll enjoy that. See you tomorrow, Sam."

"The flower garden?"

"Yes. Debbie will show you."

As Sam leaves with Debbie, Sam speaks, "Well, Debbie, Paul seems like a great guy."

"He is. I have a three-year-old, little Bryn, and my son, Ryan Gregory, just turned eighteen months. Paul doesn't mind them running around here while I work. They're with their grandparents today. My husband and I have a small ranch twenty-five miles from here. He and Paul have become good friends. Paul is so good when it comes to people. He just cares so much for others. It's contagious. He enjoys seeing others having success.

"Sam, the place I'm taking you is very special, as you'll see. It is just beyond that vine-covered wall. The entrance is tricky. See the wrought iron piece attached to the wall? Pull on that and the wall will separate."

"A secret garden?" Sam asks.

"Yes, it is." Debbie says smiling.

Sam tries pulling the handle.

"Pull a little harder. That's it. Hold it for a moment. Okay. There in the center, in front of that bench, is the flower garden he wanted me to show you."

The entire area hidden behind the vine-covered wall, filled with a variety of plants, is beautiful and well cared for. But as Sam approaches the flower garden Paul particularly wanted her to see, she exclaims: "It is beautiful! I mean, it is really beautiful. It is magnificent! I have never seen anything like this. Where did you find these flowers?"

"I don't know, but visitors are just mesmerized when they come here. He doesn't share this with everyone so you've impressed him in some sort of way. It's where Paul visits when he needs quiet time. It's the one spot where he won't allow photos to be taken. Sorry, but that's his rule. He says he wants people to enjoy the moments they are here and wants them to store those moments in their memories only. So no photos here, I must insist."

"But this may be the very photograph that would guarantee his story getting into the magazine. I mean, Debbie, I've never seen such beauty in all of my life. This is extraordinary!"

"No photos and you have to promise me that. It would cost me my job."

Chapter 5

As Sam enters the small motel, she is immediately greeted by the only person there.

"Hello Miss Hodges. Welcome to our home. While you stay with us, this is your home away from home. I am Pedro Garcia. Call me Pedro. I am here to make you as comfortable as you would be in your own home. Please sit down for a moment and enjoy the popcorn I made fresh for your arrival."

"You must not have any other visitors coming tonight given you knew my name."

"Miss Hodges, we have but six rooms, and tonight they are all filled. We are blessed! And to have such an important guest from New York as yourself, thank you. Thank you for staying here with us. I already completed the paperwork for you, and you just need to sign here. Do not worry about your credit card. We can take care of that anytime.

"In your room, I made a special treat for you, and we will have a special dessert for you before your bedtime. Also, there is a wonderful little restaurant down the street five minutes. Their menu is in your room. Just tell us what you like, and we will bring it to you. Pedro, me, will take care of everything for you. Would you like a wake-up call in the morning?"

"No thanks, Pedro."

"Then let me take you to your home for tonight. I will get your bags."

As they walk toward Sam's room, she notices the hallway is freshly painted and carpeted. The décor is western, but homey and friendly. There are paintings on the walls with scenes of Native Americans, cowboys, and local landscapes. Pedro opens her door, and Sam is pleasantly surprised as she enters her room. The room is quite spacious, painted in warm colors, very clean and tidy. It looks quite comfortable. There is a dining room table with a freshly prepared serving platter of an assortment of cheeses, crackers, nuts, fruits and bottled water. Sam doesn't see a need to order out. This is uncommon service and makes her smile.

"Pedro, you do a good job of running the motel. I'm sure I will be quite comfortable staying here. Thank you."

"You are welcome Miss Hodges. Please enjoy your stay. And do not forget; Pedro is here to take care of any need you have. Do not hesitate to call the front desk. I will be here in a jiffy."

As Sam reaches in her purse to find a couple of dollars to tip Pedro, he speaks: "No, no Miss Hodges. This is the beginning of your stay with us. Please, save your tip for when you leave. I want you to be sure all of your stay was deserving of your praise, not just the first few minutes. Keep your money. If when you leave, you feel a tip is deserved, leave something on the bed, privately. Then only an amount you feel is deserved. So keep your money safe."

"Thank you, Pedro, so much."

As Pedro leaves the room and closes the door behind him, Sam drops on the bed, kicks her shoes off, and takes a deep breath. After a couple of minutes, she calls her editor from her cell phone.

"Vince, Sam here. Can you call me when you get this message?"

Sam ponders her day: After three flights, one long layover, and then a bumpy drive to the middle of nowhere, I was already tired when I arrived. I hope I can find something to create an interest for the magazine, but I'm not optimistic. Oh well, I needed some time away from New York City. I thought I would enjoy being out here more than I have. I guess I'm a city girl at heart. Darn, the one photo I think would impress Vince, I am not able to take. Hopefully, I can get that decision changed.

Sam's cell phone rings. "Hello . . . Hi Vince . . . I wanted to report how my day went. We wrapped up our interview today, and I'm going to get some photos tomorrow. I think we may have something for the magazine. I'm sitting down now to review my notes and begin writing the article. I'll talk to you tomorrow. Talk to you then. Bye."

Actually, there's not much from which to work, but I can't tell Vince. After all, I'm here on the magazine's time and money, and I want to be as positive as possible. Besides, I want to postpone as long as possible Vince's tirade that will take place if there isn't a story.

Let's see. Marilyn, his deceased wife, was killed by a drunk driver. Paul went off the deep end and a few years later, he was hit and almost killed by a drunk driver.

While in a coma, Paul believes he visited his deceased wife in the spirit world. Paul says he was taken to her by somebody and was taught something from the spirit world. Let's see. He said something about a "newfound knowledge he learned while visiting her." Yeah, right. I can see telling that to Vince. I'd be the laughing stock of the office.

Well, like I've read and heard about many times, he came back from a near-death experience with newfound enthusiasm for life. I accept he had a near-death experience. I don't believe he left his body, and I certainly don't believe he communicated with the dead. I believe science is pretty clear the brain has the ability to have electrical misfires when the body is starting to shut down and can make one hallucinate and believe those out-of-body experiences are taking place.

In fact, I saw a study where the scientist was able to duplicate the out-of-body experience in subjects by stimulating electrodes in the part of the brain that controls hallucinations. Those participants believed they had visited the "light" and left their bodies.[2]

Now, he did come back from standing on a street corner begging for money to having built a company from the ground up, with virtually no investment capital, to a business doing nearly fifty million dollars in annual revenue. He now earns weekly more than the average American earns annually. This took him just a few short years. He accomplished this with an average education, no special skills, and was inspired by overhearing a conversation in a McDonald's restaurant.

He said he didn't do this just for himself, but to benefit his community by helping those who were homeless possess their own part of the American dream. We didn't even cover that. After all, that's what brought me here. Maybe there's more here than I found today. My brain just wasn't working that well after the arduous trip.

How did he turn his life around so impressively? Here's something. He said something about discussing later those low-paying jobs. That seemed important to him. He said the tragedy of being hit and almost killed was a grand experience in his life. We should cover that. And what is that "newfound knowledge" he mentioned? Did I not pay attention there? Also, he said he heard the magic words "residual income" from a conversation in McDonald's. Maybe I should ask him more about that. Indeed, I need to get some sleep and start over tomorrow.

Chapter 6

It is well to be up before daybreak for such habits
Contribute to health, wealth, and wisdom.
—Aristotle, BC 384-322 BC
Greek Philosopher, poet,
Student of Plato,
Teacher to Alexander the Great

Paul thinking to himself: I wake up automatically every morning at 4:30. I love the mornings. It is still dark when I awaken. I will get my coffee that Lisa, the house computer, has fixed for me. Then I go to my office overlooking the pool which looks as if it touches the distant mountains. The sun rising over the eastern slopes gives the illusion gold has been poured everywhere. By the time the sun is showing its glory, I've had my coffee, read the various highlights from the newspaper I subscribe to over the internet, checked my emails, product orders, and commission report. I'll have showered, changed into my workout clothes, and if the weather permits, I'll have prepared for my morning run across my slice of heaven.

I love life, and I no longer fear it'll all be taken from me. It is great in every way. What a glorious day! How different I feel than in those months and years following Marilyn's death.

Debbie comes in at 8 a.m. Usually, her daughter, Bryn, and little Ryan will be with her. Debbie does all of the housekeeping, some garden work, and tends to other detail work. Her efforts allow me to do what I do best—help develop the skills in others to help them build their own American dream.

I've left this day wide open in anticipation the interview with Sam was going to creep into a second day. Apparently, I overestimated my interesting and successful life. Sam did not seem too impressed.

24

However, I am impressed with Sam, her no-nonsense approach to her business, insightful questions, not to speak of her impressive stature. I hope to see her before she leaves regardless of whether she has any additional questions for me.

"Good morning, Debbie. Hi, Bryn. Hi, Ryan."

"Good morning, Paul."

"Hi, Mr. Fisher. Can I have a chocolate?"

"Bryn, you know you have to ask your mommy if that is okay."

Bryn is so smart and personable. She loves playing with her dolls, dressing up, and posing for the camera. I wouldn't be a bit surprised if she were to find her way into entertainment.

"Paul, there's a message on the phone from Sam. She wants to see you around nine-thirty if that works for you. She says she has some additional questions for you."

"That's fine. Give her a call and tell her I'll see her then."

"Think about this: When our forefathers came to this land, what kind of people were they? They were people who wanted to come to a place where they had freedom to pursue their dreams, where their courage and willingness to take risks would be rewarded, and where they could pursue a life of meaning and adventure; that was in their DNA. Sure, there are people all over the world with this special DNA, but it is in abundance here in our country!"

"I never thought of it that way. I guess that does separate us from others."

"Yes. It's not the time management tricks, organizational skills, or the discipline taught by efficiency experts. Many of them don't have uncommon success. Yet, many who have uncommon success don't have those skills. You can hire people with organizational skills. Don't get me wrong; you'll see there are important skills anyone can learn to help them realize their dreams."

"Paul, you seem to have been able to succeed despite not having the right education, the right school, the right fraternity . . . maybe even not having the right pedigree for success. What sets you apart?"

"The beauty of this country is we can each decide what path we want to take regardless of who our parents are. Make no mistake; I'm proud of my parents. But it's not a Harvard education, an MBA degree, or having the right family, or the right contacts that makes you who you are. For some of us, our education has come from other sources: the people we meet, life experience, the internet, the library, and even from beyond."

"Uh, beyond?"

"Sam, you have an outstanding education, great looks, a bright mind, a great career; but are you filled with joy? Do you feel right now you have uncommon success? It's not my business, but if you don't, you should be sitting there wanting to know every detail of what I'm talking about, and why life is so spectacular for me and many of those I've taught. You should open your heart and let my words pour into your soul."

"Paul, you have my attention. I want to hear your story as you believe it to be true. I really do. Let's start where you were hit by the drunk driver, and your spirit leaves your body. Is that a good place to begin?"

Chapter 8

Whom do I call educated?
First, those who manage well the circumstances
They encounter day by day.
Next, those who are decent and honorable in their
Intercourse with all men, bearing easily and good naturedly
What is offensive in others and being as agreeable
And reasonable to their associates as is possible to be . . .
Those who hold their pleasures always under control
And are not ultimately overcome by their misfortunes . . .
Those who are not spoiled by their successes,
Who do not desert their true selves, but
Held their ground steadfastly as wise and sober minded men.
—Socrates, 469 BC-399 BC
Greek philosopher,
Teacher to Plato,
One of founders of Western Philosophy

I wasn't expecting this turn of events. Am I ready to do this? I've shared my "secrets to success" with all of my associates, and the success stories are plentiful as a result. But I haven't said where these principles originated. Here goes what I hope is the right time and place to share all of what I know . . . or at least most of it.

"Okay Sam, let's go for it. Well, as I mentioned, my spirit left my mangled body to escape the pain. I was sure my mortal existence was over; at least that is what I was hoping. After watching the EMTs work on me in the street and then being taken into the ambulance, I visited my siblings instantly. I wanted to ease their pain as they learned of my accident. Of

course, they didn't know my spirit was with them. Then, this person or personage came to me, and I could tell without words he was taking me to where I needed to go. It was in this beautiful place where I knew I was surrounded by love and perfection.

"As I told you, the beauty was beyond description. I was shown my life in its fullness, saw all of my mistakes which were considerable, and felt the pain for not only what I did, but for what I could've done, but failed to do. Specifically, I could've lived a life with joy even after the loss of my most precious love, Marilyn. What I learned was the more one is able to accomplish in this life, the more one can do to help others. It's not about what we can do for ourselves. It's about service to others, and for me that meant helping others reach their potential. I learned, Sam, if you seek to love others without qualification, then serving others is what you want to do. It becomes the evidence of the love which fills your heart.

"Now, there are many ways to be of service to others. My way is to help people find the joy I have. You see, I learned a life lived selflessly helping others is a life rewarded. We all want rewarded and the greatest reward is when we are helping others and for me, helping others reach their goals. What we do for others comes back a thousand times. Look what I have here while living to help others. So, by helping others achieve what they want, we end up achieving more than we could ever achieve living life selfishly. Serving others comes back spiritually, emotionally and, yes, financially. But, until you find your own purpose, living life to its fullest is difficult."

"Paul, I would like to hear about your meeting with Marilyn—though that is still difficult to say. Uh, yes, let's talk about your conversation with your deceased wife in her new home up there in the clouds. How is that? I am trying, Paul."

"I've had my own issues with this, believe me. But let me share with you what I believe. As I said, the messenger took me to this very beautiful and peaceful place. She was there. I could see her in every detail just like the day I saw her for the first time. This time, however, she was even more beautiful if that is possible. Her love for me was even greater than it was on earth. She spoke in her perfect and beautiful voice just as she'd always done. I spoke to her with my voice just as always. The messenger stayed nearby, and the one thing I knew without having to be told was that he knew what each of us felt or thought without our having to say anything. If I thought it, he knew it. Then, Marilyn spoke to me."

"Paul, come, sit. I wasn't expecting you. But I promise you, we'll make the best of these moments no matter how little time we have."

"What do you mean how little time we have? I want to spend an eternity with you."

"Paul," she said calmly and purposefully. "I want you to return to where you belong. I don't believe you're meant to stay in this state, and I plan to help you prepare for your return."

"Prepare for what? I want to be here with you more than anything," I said.

"And I promise you that time will come, and it will be like the blink of an eye. The emotions you're feeling are evidence this isn't your time. I believe you're here because there's something I can teach you that will help you make your life what it should be."

Then she said: "You have lost your way, but together we'll get you back on the path you were intended to walk. Do you remember the dreams you once had? The life we were going to have together? The home we were going to build, the children we were going to have, all of what we were to have together?"

"Yes, of course. I can't get you out of my mind." I said.

"Your dreams must change, but you can still live your dreams. However, you must trust me that I know how to help you. Will you let me help you?"

"I said I was ready, but I just wanted to be with Marilyn. With that, we began what I would eventually call the 'Seven Secrets to Live Life Abundantly.' Sam, are you ready for this journey?"

Chapter 9

If one advances confidently
In the direction of his dreams
And endeavors to live the life which he has imagined,
He will meet with a success unexpected in common hours.
If you have built castles in the air
Your work need not be lost.
That is where they should be.
Now put foundations under them.
—Henry David Thoreau, 1817-1862
American author, poet, philosopher, naturalist, tax resister

Marilyn speaking to Paul, "Paul, here is the first principle . . .

Believe You Already Have the Things You Want,
And You Will Have Those Things.

"This is where the magic begins to happen," Marilyn continues:

"Paul, you must learn to use your mind's eye to see what you can't see. Andrew Carnegie said that 'whatever a man can conceive and believe, he can achieve.'[3] Your mind's eye is not a visual eye; it is an eye of belief and faith.

"By the way, Andrew told me when he was a teenager and earned his first paycheck, a whopping thirty-five dollars working for a telegraph company, he showed the check to a friend. He said to his friend, 'I am the wealthiest man in the world!'[4] He was already putting to work this important principle. He already had in his minds' eye or his metaphysical world if you will, what he would eventually have in the physical world. That's how this principle works."

"You have spoken with Andrew Carnegie?"

"Yes, Paul."

"Paul," Marilyn continues. "Do you remember the time when we were together, and we had special-ordered a new fish aquarium for our apartment? It would be six weeks before we received it, but we moved furniture, made a spot for it, and purchased the necessary accessories. Even though we didn't have the aquarium, we knew it was coming, and we prepared for it. It works similarly with the dreams we have. We must begin preparing and acting as if we already have what we are dreaming about. To have something tomorrow, you must first believe you have it now. It's in that realm of the metaphysical that the magic begins to work."

"Sam, it's even biblical. Jesus instructed, 'Believe that the things you ask for you already have, and you will have.'[5] There are certain laws that go beyond what science can measure, and this is one of those laws. I will repeat that because it is so important: 'Believe that the things you ask for you already have, and you will have.'"

Sam says, "Paul, I think I know what you are saying. A few years ago, I can remember meeting an American gun engraver. He was a great artist who could put his art work to steel. I believe his name was L.C. something.[6] The characters he engraved on steel looked life-like whether it was a hunter, a bird, an elephant, or whatever. I asked him how he did that.

"He said he could not begin a project until he could see the result in his mind. Then, to bring it to life, the secret was in the eye of the character, whether it was a hunter or an animal he was engraving, ever so tiny as it might be. He said the eye was the last thing he engraved on each character. It was just two or three taps with his hammer to his specially-designed chisel that made the difference, but until his mind's eye could see the life in the character, he could not put the hammer to the chisel. Sometimes it would take two or three days before he could make those taps with his hammer. Once he saw it in his mind's eye, it was easy to put it to the steel."[7]

"Sam, the mind's eye is important. We must see it first before we can actually have it manifested. Are you familiar with the comedic actor Jim Carrey?"

"Yes."

"Here is a story he has told about himself. While a struggling stand-up comedian in 1987 without any money, he drove his old, beat-up Toyota to a scenic overview of Los Angeles. As he sat there dreaming and pondering his future, he saw a scrap of paper on the floor of his car. From the glove box, he took a pen and he drew a facsimile of a check payable to him for ten million dollars, and dated it for Thanksgiving, 1995, eight years into his future. He made a notation on the check 'for acting services rendered.' He carefully folded the scrap of paper that now looked like a check and placed it in his wallet where he would regularly take it out and read it.

"Whether he knew it or not, he was practicing this principle. There was only one problem; I guess he underestimated inflation. Instead of being paid the ten million dollars he had dreamed about, that he had written on the scrap of paper, and that he had regularly visualized . . . he was paid twenty million dollars for 'acting services rendered' nearly to the date he had written on his makeshift check. He saw it in his mind's eye; he believed it and made it real."[8]

Marilyn continues speaking to me, "Paul, put together a prayer that speaks to this principle. Express thanks for the things you want as if you have them already, and you will have them. You will learn the principles to make this a reality."

"So I constructed this prayer:

> *Thank You for the blessings of my outstanding health, for my ability to run without pain, for the strength to work each day with passion and purpose. Thank You for the wonderful woman in my life and for the children who have blessed us. Thank You for the continued increased knowledge of the important principles to live a life of introspection, integrity, empathy, and service. Thank You for the business that you have guided me toward that allows me to benefit and serves so many. Thank You for the financial abundance my efforts have attracted from being of service to others. Thank You for the beautiful home in the part of the country that we have always wanted to live. Thank You for this life and the opportunity to share our love, joy and happiness with all we come in contact. For this I have received, I am eternally grateful. Thank You."*

The last sentence says 'For this I HAVE received . . . .' Now remember, at that time I had none of those things. I was racked in so much pain I was out of my body. Marilyn was only with me until I went back into my body which was by now comatose at the hospital. I had no woman in my life, had no children, my health was nonexistent, and I had no money to my name and certainly was in no position to be a blessing to anyone. I had been standing on street corners taking from others, and I'd not been a blessing to anyone.

"But, I was instructed to be thankful for all of those things as if I already had them. I had to believe I had all of those things I wanted and then, I would have them. I did what I was told. I wasn't back in my body yet; but all of these things that were being taught to me were firmly planted in my mind, and I knew they were true, and I was going to do them."

"Paul, this prayer is supposed to change your life? So, all of us who do not believe in a God who orchestrates these things are left to fail? I know plenty of people who have had a great deal of success who do not believe in God. How do you explain that if all of this is true?"

"I have met those same people. I am not saying only believers are meant to live life abundantly. I do believe there are people who are 'wired for success.' Now, these are simply those folks who never lost that innate knowledge of those ingredients for uncommon success. Some of us just have to work harder at it than others, but all can have it. These principles work for everyone, even if you don't know they are working. Andrew Carnegie didn't limit his important message to only some. These are lessons for each of us."

"Paul, many wealthy, happy, and wonderfully successfully people when asked to describe what caused them to be so successful attribute it to two things: luck and hard work. Isn't that what really determines one's success? That maybe there's a certain 'serendipity' to how one's life turns out?"

"Sam, it's more than that. Even with those people who say that, when asked enough questions would begin saying some other things. They might say they believe in themselves, they have a passion for what they are doing, an enthusiasm for getting it done, the persistence and unwillingness to fail despite the obstacles in front of them; and they have a dogged determination to do what has to be done now.

"What I was being taught was how best to harness all of that and then some. When you know there is a purpose to your efforts, and you know the results of your efforts are not just possible, but are guaranteed, and the truth of that goes back centuries; then you can remain enthusiastic, passionate, and persistent during the difficult times. When you have the principles, you will have everything else.

"Having said that, I did come to believe how my late wife, Marilyn, the spirit teaching me all of these things, came to know what she did. So let me ask you, Sam, these questions. If there was one particular philosopher who spoke his entire life on how to live life abundantly, and this one philosopher was considered by many to be the greatest of all philosophers when it came to understanding how to live successfully; would you want to listen to him?"

"Of course, if I was convinced he had something to say to my life, I'd want to listen."

"Would you incorporate his instructions into your life?"

"Probably."

"Probably? See what I mean? Not everyone is ready to change his—or maybe her—life. Now, what if there was a Creator of the Universe? If there was a Creator of you and me, wouldn't you want His instructions, on how to live life abundantly? Loaded question, huh? I believe that would be the source I'd be most interested hearing tell me how I can be joyful and successful. Sam, just stay with me on this; you've not heard anything yet. Principle 1 is:

Believe You Already Have the Things You Want, And You will Have Those Things.

"So, I did what Marilyn instructed me to do."

She said: "Each morning I want you to recite the prayer. I want you to create this prayer that speaks to all the dreams you have, the person you want to be, and the causes you want to pursue to help others. You must know these things you want have already been given to you and will manifest themselves to you in time. This prayer is to express gratitude for the things you want and believe you already have. And Paul, I want you to read this aloud to yourself. I want you to hear your prayer from your voice."

My Prayer of Gratitude for the Things

Received But Not Yet Seen

Chapter 10

Principle 2

All that we are is the result of what we have thought.
If a man speaks or acts with an evil thought, pain follows him.
If a man speaks or acts with a pure thought, happiness follows him,
Like a shadow that never leaves him.
—Siddhartha Gotama Buddha, 563 BCE-483 BCE
Founder and the Supreme Leader of Buddhism

"Sam, when Marilyn speaks, the person I think of as the messenger is always nearby. I quickly came to understand he was more than a messenger; he was Marilyn's mentor in this new home of hers. All she said was with his approval. He was not an unwanted presence; quite the opposite, his presence was comforting. I moved him in my mind from 'The Messenger' to 'The Mentor.' He seemed to smile as I had this thought in my mind.

"Marilyn tells me I have to lift my spirit outward and open my heart to the possibilities life holds. But I must be willing to take full responsibility for everything that happens in my life. And the greatest evidence of what I've ever had, currently have, or ever will have is the result of something we all do every single day and give little thought to the results. So the second principle I was to learn was something I never heard before. The Second Principle is:

Change Your Words and You Will Change Your Life.

"What does that mean?" I asked.

Marilyn continues her teachings: "Words matter. In fact, life and death, healing and sickness, prosperity and poverty, all are controlled by the words you speak.[9] Let me say that again. Your words, not your thoughts, control your life. Speak of negativity and you'll invite negativity. Speak optimistically and you'll attract good things. Speak to your fears and they'll come to pass. If you say you can't do it, you can't."

I interjected, "Henry Ford said something similar, 'whether you think you can or you think you can't, you are right.'[10] He said that.

"I thought that was pretty good."

Marilyn said. "Yes, Paul, Henry told me that, but it's what you speak that really matters."

I said, "He told you personally, Henry Ford?"

Marilyn continues: "Your life events cannot rise above the words you speak. In fact, you are the sum total of what you have said about yourself, your life, and your circumstances. Your words must rise to the life you want. Your words are giving you the life you have."[11]

"Paul," Sam says, "If that's true, that's very powerful. I want to make sure I've written down what you said, 'Your words must rise to the life you want. Your words are giving you the life you have.' That is quite interesting."

"I agree. After Marilyn spoke, I remembered reading a book that documented this idea. The book called 'Learned Optimism' was written by Martin Seligman, PhD.[12] In his book, there was a chapter on sports events and the conversations of the athletes after losses. Dr. Seligman followed the winningest baseball teams and basketball teams for an entire year after their winning seasons. He also tracked the worst teams in each of those sports the following year.

"He would read the quotes of players and coaches of each of these teams in the various sports publications following a loss. He figured a loss tends to bring out the raw emotions of the players and coaches. He developed a system of grading the comments from optimistic to pessimistic. It soon became apparent he could actually predict a win or a loss for the following game as a result of either how optimistic or pessimistic the comments made after a loss.

"For example, if the team members said after a loss, 'we just fell apart down the stretch' . . . or, 'we get killed every time a game is on the line,' that team very likely would lose the next game; or at least it would not cover the spread he used to equal out the difference between the talent of the teams.

"On the other hand, if the team made comments like, 'you have to give our opponent credit, they just played a great game, but we're fine' . . . or:

41

'That happens. You can't win them all.' Those comments would bode well for the team winning its next game. This formula, grading the words spoken by players and coaches after a loss, allowed Dr. Seligman to predict the results of the next game successfully into the seventy-fifth percentile."[13]

"Paul, how is that study relevant to the average person who is not a professional athlete?"

"I would ask a person, what are you saying to yourself, your family or your friends when you feel defeated? In other words, what raw emotion is coming from your tongue when life is not treating you as well as you'd like? Then, correct your words if they aren't giving you what you want.

"I would warn parents: How many children will spend their lifetimes overcoming the unintentional but harmful things their parents said to them believing they were helping them? That is how we lose that 'program for success' we each brought into this world. Our ancestors were achievers, risk-takers, optimists, and we have that in our DNA!"

"So Paul, you believe that by simply speaking the right way you can affect your life in a positive way?"

"Yes, I do. Words mean something and they are contagious. They will influence individuals, groups, teams, businesses, communities, and even countries. They influenced our nation in 1980 as then-presidential-candidate Ronald Reagan spoke to the American people about the possibilities our great nation held despite double-digit unemployment and double-digit inflation. As president, he restored the confidence of the American people in themselves and restored the confidence of the world in America. Also, think of just how important his words were to the world when he said, 'Mr. Gorbachev, tear down this wall.'

"Here's another example: Sam, if you turn to the pages of Genesis in the Old Testament, you'll see that our world was created through the spoken word. You'll see a lot of 'And God *said* . . . and it was so.' He didn't think it; He said it. So let's say you don't believe the Bible and those were just words chosen for the story of creation. Someone recognized it requires spoken words to make things happen. Whatever our goals, we must first speak to those goals.

"The late Napoleon Hill[14] wrote the book, 'Think and Grow Rich,' a great book, although I believe it would've been more accurate to name it, 'Speak and Grow Rich.' Our thoughts take no action until we speak to them. What should be comforting is to know that our thoughts aren't keeping us from achieving success. When we're thinking in a negative way, we can correct that with our words. We are in control.

"In fact, your death or your life, your failure or your success, your sickness or your health, all are in the power of your spoken word—not God's, not fate, not serendipity. You have total control."

Sam asks, "Paul, if death and life are in the power of our spoken words, the words we speak, you are implying that God—for those who believe in Him—doesn't determine when we die. We determine that. Isn't this contrary to what most people believe? Even Christians?"

"Here's what I know: By following what ends up being seven principles Marilyn has taught me, I've changed everything about my life and the lives of many around me. You can judge for yourself the results.

"Sam, I'm thinking that The Creator, God, has put us in charge of our lives. He's not a micromanager. He has endowed us with the responsibility to determine our own destiny. However, and this is important: *I have come to believe that when we are doing what we were destined to do and which is pleasing to Him, doors open that would have been closed, opportunities arise that otherwise would not have, and we are protected and guided.*[15] I believe that to be true.

"He has created us after Himself; we can achieve uncommon joy and a life of abundance while on this earth, and we carry our experiences and knowledge to the next eternal existence. I believe He is happiest when we are joyful and living life full. Jesus, whom many believe to be the Son of God, was teaching his followers how to live this life—not just preparing for eternal life. This I know."

"Paul, there are a lot of great thinkers who don't believe in a Creator, let alone His 'only begotten Son' having walked among us."

"I believe you can be a very smart person, with an incredibly high IQ, and not be an open-minded person to the possibility that the reason there is purpose and order to the universe is because of a much greater intelligence than ours; and our limits as human beings cannot with reason alone comprehend that power. That requires faith and there are some smart people who haven't exercised their power of faith.

"Yet, Sam, there are great thinkers who believe in God and that believing in God takes nothing away from science. Some believe Jesus was God in the flesh. Regardless, let's take for a moment Jesus, the man. His words are well documented. Let me share with you what one of our country's greatest thinkers, Thomas Jefferson, said about Him.

"First Sam, let me share with you a story about President Kennedy. When he was in the White House, he had gathered the leaders in science, the greatest scientists from around the world for a scientific summit. He said to them, 'This is the greatest collection of intelligence ever assembled here in the White House . . . except maybe for when Thomas Jefferson was here and ate alone.'[16] Thomas Jefferson is that highly regarded.

"Thomas Jefferson, one of our most important founding fathers and Presidents, was a great historian, reader, and thinker. You may be aware that when the Library of Congress burned to the ground it was Thomas Jefferson who donated his quite significant collection of books to the United States to replace much of what was lost.

"Thomas Jefferson was also a writer. One of his works became known as the 'Jeffersonian Bible' which was, in essence, all of Jesus' quotes dismantled from the New Testament. Thomas Jefferson didn't believe all of what was said by others in regard to Jesus because much of what was said was written years, decades, maybe even centuries later. Jefferson believed he could discern between what he considered fact and fiction. It is not my intention to debate that.

"However, Jefferson believed Jesus was without doubt the greatest philosopher in all of history, above Socrates, Plato and Aristotle, above every thinker of the past and up to his, Jefferson's, time. He believed no thinker in history compared to the words and philosophy of Jesus. In fact, he believed Jesus' every word was Truth."

"Paul, what do you believe when it comes to Jesus and the claim He was the Son of God?"

"Good question, Sam. Maybe I'll ask you what you think about that later.

"This I have come to believe: It seems to me the important common tenants of the three great religions teach us: To worship but one God, to love one another, to live lives that are moral, to practice repentance, to seek redemption, and to love and serve our fellow brothers and sisters without being a respecter of persons. Biblical scholars agree that Abraham was the founder of monotheism. Most biblical scholars agree that Moses, Mohammad, and Jesus were great historical figures and prophets of God. Many would add others such as Jacob, Isaac, Ishmael, and probably Enoch to the list of prophets. The members of the Church of Jesus Christ of Latter-Day-Saints would add Joseph Smith as well as the subsequent leaders of its Faith to that list. There is room for respectful disagreement, but all of these men are revered in religious history.

"Here is what I believe to be important: Whether one is Jewish, Muslim, or Christian, he or she believes in and worships the same God, namely the God of Abraham. When we learn how to respect and love one another and recognize we are brothers and sisters with the same history, then we can concentrate on making 'heaven on earth' as it was intended. This I learned."

"Wouldn't that be great? Paul, let's get back to the concept of changing our words. This idea that we have such power in our words is quite scary. It takes me back to my teenage years. My father for years spoke about his fear of having cancer even though there was no evidence of such. I will never forget his words for years before his death as he would say he could see a cancer eating at him. We even told him he should not talk that way.

"He died from cancer. I know a lot of people die from cancer, but it was as if he was giving power to that idea and sure enough, it germinated and killed him. If what you are saying is true, he was speaking death to his life, wasn't he? I wonder how many of us unwittingly do that?"

"You are right; he was speaking death to his life. He just didn't know, like most people don't know, the importance and the gravity of his own words. It's a choice. It becomes a habit, either a good one or a bad one. We are either lifting ourselves and others around us, or we are doing the opposite.

"Now, understand this. Our words are the evidence of what's in our heart. But it can be like the chicken or the egg and which came first. Does our heart change our words, or do our words change our heart? I am not sure, but I was instructed to 'change your words and you will change your life;' and it is my spoken words that determine my life or my death, my success or my failure, my good health or my sickness, a life of uncommon success or a life of despair.

"I knew I had to follow these principles if I was going to get this second chance at life. I knew Marilyn's purpose at that time and space was to teach me these things, and I wasn't going to disappoint her. And I was confident she was being coached by The Mentor.

"So, Sam, I did what Marilyn instructed me. After Marilyn made this principle known to me, she continued:"

"So, Paul, here is what you must first do to put this powerful principle to its application. I want you to write your personal mission statement.

This mission statement will give you inspiration and purpose. Without purpose guiding you, without a clear mission inspiring you, failure is certain.

"I want you to write this statement to reflect all you want to become, the principles that will guide you in your life, the way you want to treat others, and the service you will provide to give your life importance. Seek to write a statement that gives you inspiration, gives you a greater purpose in your life, and creates a passion and reason for your being.

"Then I want you to read that aloud every morning. Change your words, and you will change your life. You must *hear* the words you want to inspire and change your life. If you don't feel inspired when hearing them, rewrite them. That is important."

"So I began to write:

> *"My mission and my purpose in this life are to serve, inspire, and help as many people as I come in contact with, both in my business and in my personal life. To find a partner I can share my life with, to have children we can love and help grow in knowledge and faith. To become financially independent while giving to charities regularly. To build a home that will inspire our family and encourage our friends. To live a life seeking truth and knowledge, to live with integrity and honesty, to treat others with the same respect, empathy, and love I want in return. To find a profession in which I can be passionate, and one in which I can teach and persuade others to attain their dreams. To share ideas and concepts that inspire and lift those around me. To live a life as closely to my ideals and principles as I possibly can. To grow spiritually and provide something each and every day that helps others. This is my mission; this is my purpose.*

"That's what I wrote down then. I've changed it over these years, but the idea is the same. My goals to serve just keep getting bigger. I review my mission statement regularly and change it as it needs to be changed. I was committed to following this principle:"

Change Your Words and You Will Change Your Life.

My Mission Statement to Guide My New Path

Chapter 11

Principle 3

> *For verily I say unto you,*
> *That whosoever shall say unto this mountain,*
> *Be thou removed, and be thou cast into the sea;*
> *And shall not doubt in his heart,*
> *But shall believe that those things*
> *Which he saith shall come to pass;*
> *He shall have whatsoever he saith.*
> —Mark 11: 23

Marilyn speaks, "For your third principle, you must learn to:

Harness the Power of Hope, Faith, and Works.

"Paul, let's look at how these three concepts work together.

"First, there's an important relationship between 'hope' and 'faith.' *Hope* represents your dreams. *Faith* is the *substance* of what you hope for. Without faith, your hopes—dreams—will die. When a person loses hope he may feel he has nothing to live for.

"You must hold onto your dreams tightly. You've lost yours and you must find them again. You must have faith or your dreams will slip away. If you want to make your dreams a physical reality in your life, you must activate your faith. So hope without faith is simply hopes or dreams that will never be realized and will disappear in a sea of despair."

I ask Marilyn, "How do you activate faith?"

She continues: "You do it with your *works*. Just like there is a relationship between hope and faith, there is also a relationship between 'faith' and 'works.' Works are the *evidence* of your faith. Remember, faith is real. It is the substance of your hopes. But faith without works disappears. What does that mean to you, Paul?" Marilyn asks.

"It tells me that our works—the efforts we put toward anything—are important to activating our faith. Without works, our faith will diminish until we can't see the proverbial 'light at the end of the tunnel.'[17] I guess that's where I am."

"That is a pretty fair assessment, Paul. The power of this trilogy of 'hope, faith, and works' is in the realization that you must exercise these concepts together: *Faith is the substance of hope. The work you put forth toward achieving your hopes and dreams is evidence of your faith that you can and will achieve your hopes and dreams.*

"Nothing will manifest itself to you during your lifetime without your working toward that manifestation. If one says he or she has faith in anything, then his or her works, or effort, or how he or she lives, should evidence that claim of faith. The three must work for you together."

I said to Marilyn, "like the three musketeers: 'all for one, one for all!'"

Sam says: "Paul, what you're saying makes sense to me. When I was growing up, my father used to say, 'What you do speaks so loudly, I can't hear what you say.' He insisted I always work hard, and I always have been a hard worker. He said constantly, 'hard work trumps everything.' In school, I wanted to have the highest grades. In my career, I've always wanted to be the best reporter. Consequently, work has always played an important role in my life. Had I been a person who said 'yes, I know hard work pays off,' yet I never worked hard, then I probably lacked the faith that hard work paid off."

Paul responds: "Sam, it's not about *hard* work. It's about purposeful work, inspired work; work that's intended to make your dreams your reality. We all know people who've worked very hard all of their lives, hated what they did and, consequently, never lived a life of uncommon success. With an economy that has plenty of unemployed, they feel lucky to have a job and are able to pay their bills, so they've limited their hopes to equal their circumstances. Why rock the boat when it's floating fine?' they may argue.

"Remember, most people settle for their circumstances and adjust their expectations accordingly. They deserve respect and should be honored because they've given up their lives for their families. However, Marilyn was providing me this course on living an abundant life, fulfilled, happy, with uncommon love and service to others. That's what I wanted."

"Paul," Sam says: "On the other hand, we all know people who've grown accustomed to living on government handouts. They've lost all hope. There are millions of them."

Paul responds: "Many of those people have talents to offer if they only were able to learn these principles. I've proof of that in my own organization. Work ethic changes when people have faith their hopes and dreams can be realized. That is when work becomes what it's supposed to be—fulfilling one's destiny and even fun."

Sam asks, "How does one do that, harness this power of hope, faith, and works?"

Wow, Paul says to himself. Is this a breakthrough? Sam may have just taken the first step toward wanting to know how she can benefit from what, until now, she probably thought was a fairy tale. Her question was genuine.

"Sam, here is what I learned: Some of the homeless families I have been able to help were at a very low point in life. Some were so far removed from living the life they once dreamed that they had given up on themselves. They can't see what their talent is, what assets they may have, and have lost sight of their dreams. Just earning a paycheck can be a huge lift in their confidence and can begin opening up their hearts to possibilities. I was once like them after Marilyn died and before I was critically injured and went through this crash course—no pun intended—on how to live life abundantly. Let me get back to Marilyn's message and try to answer your question."

Marilyn continues: "Aristotle said about achieving uncommon success: 'First, you must have a definite goal, an objective. Second, have the necessary means to achieve your end—that is, wisdom, money, materials, and methods. Third, adjust all of your means to that end.'"

"He told you personally?" I asked Marilyn.

"He did. But therein lies the answer as to how to harness the power of hope, faith, and works: The action plan for this principle is all about changing your hopes and dreams into goals, organizing those goals, determining what assets you have or will need to accomplish them, and setting into motion your action plan to achieve those goals."

"Sam, here is the process Marilyn taught me: First, let your imagination run wild and write down all of your hopes and dreams, as many as you like. I wanted to write a list of at least 100 goals with no limits. Some important, some fun. So, I just dreamed away and wrote all that I dreamed.

"Second, organize those goals into seven categories. I learned that a balanced life needed nourishment in each of these categories and all of your goals will fall into one or more of these. They are:

1. *Emotional or personal goals*
2. *Physical goals (aerobic, strength, endurance, flexibility, and lean body mass fitness)*
3. *Social goals (developing and strengthening relationships and hosting and attending events)*
4. *Spiritual goals (reading scriptures and strengthening faith)*
5. *Family goals (relationship-building, family time and trips)*
6. *Financial goals (income and asset planning and goal-setting*
7. *Business goals (activities associated with growing and developing revenue)*

"If upon organizing your goals you find you have very few or maybe none listed in one or more of the seven categories, you may want to consider why. You may want to add goals you hadn't thought of before.

"Each of these seven categories represents the areas of our lives we need to nourish. I think of these seven important areas of our lives as seven fuel tanks. We are always burning fuel from each of these tanks. Each of these fuel tanks needs to be refilled regularly. Sometimes we let one of the tanks get nearly empty. Then, it is important we spend the time and effort to refill that tank."

"Third, determine what you must have in the way of assets to make that goal a reality in your life. Aristotle said you must have the 'necessary means' to accomplish your goal. What are 'necessary means?' Is it knowledge you don't currently have? Money? The right business? You must determine what it is. If you already have what you need, great! If not, use your imagination to determine what course of action you need to take to accomplish your goal. Remember, imagination is unlimited. That's why it is one of your greatest sources for everything you do.

"Finally, take steps each day toward achieving your important goals. With your newfound knowledge of how to harness the power of hope, faith and works, nothing will hold you back."

"Paul, give me an example of an *emotional goal.*"

"Let's say you wanted to overcome the fear of speaking before groups. You decided to join a Toastmasters International Club[18] to overcome that fear and become a confident speaker. That might be an emotional goal because it's overcoming a fear, building confidence and adding to your self-esteem."

"Paul, I'm guessing that those 'bucket lists' are filled with personal goals?"

"Probably. If it will make you feel good, it's probably an emotional or a personal goal. Say you want to visit Hawaii. That would be a personal goal. Take your family to Hawaii, a family goal. Each of your goals may fall into more than one category, but there is usually one category that it dominates."

"Can one start with the seven categories and simply write down his goals for each category instead of categorizing them after his goals have been written?"

"I am sure that works just fine. Whichever way allows you to begin the process is perfectly fine. Here's what I did: In no particular order, I began scribbling my dreams to paper.

Visit Rome, Paris, Alaska . . . have a radio show . . . finish my degree . . . a graduate degree . . . help one person turn his life into financial success, help ten, then one hundred . . . sail through the Panama Canal . . . see the aurora borealis . . . read the Old and New Testaments . . . get physically fit . . . read ten biographies of great Americans . . . earn a hundred thousand dollars . . . a million dollars . . . help someone else earn a million dollars . . . run a marathon . . . provide college education to my nephews and nieces . . . clean and paint my garage . . . organize my closets . . . become financially independent . . . jump from an airplane . . . climb Mt. McKinley . . . host a party of 100 people . . . be a leader in business, etcetera. So the list grew as I jumped from dream to dream, some way out there while others were just a chore I needed to do.

"After I listed more than a hundred goals for my lifetime, I went back and organized them into each category: emotional or personal, spiritual, social, physical, family, financial, and business goals. Then I placed a number next to the goals. 'One' for goals I wanted to achieve this year;

'three' for three-year goals, five, ten and, finally, a lifetime. Then, I ranked the goals by importance for my one-year goals. That showed me what I had to do right now!

"You must determine what you must do to accomplish the goal. Each goal will require some kind of sacrifice. Then you must determine if the sacrifice is worth the goal. When you begin working toward a goal, describe that goal on paper in every detail—the more detail the better. Visit that image often. Take a page or more for the important goals you are going to work toward first. Take a picture of the house you want in a neighborhood you want to live in. Describe the features you want it to have. Make it real in your mind's eye.

"I prioritized by importance and then determined what I must do this year, this month, this week, this day, and this morning to accomplish that goal. By writing these down, your hopes become goals. With my newfound knowledge, I had faith I could make these come to pass. Then, by giving myself a plan of action, I was going to create the work to be evidence of my faith these things will come to pass."

"Didn't you feel overwhelmed at first?"

"No, not really. I included goals that would be relatively easy to accomplish. I wanted to see success right away in order to become accomplished at goal-setting and achieving."

"Take little steps first. Set your goals in stages that you can manage. If your goal is financial in nature, where do you want to be five years from now, three years, in one year? What must you do this year, this month, this week, this day, and this morning to make that happen?

"Make each goal one that excites you, creates passion, and keeps you interested as you focus on that goal every day. Look at what you have written regularly. Treat each goal that way.

"When you study the seven categories of goals, you will see some categories in which you may need very little concentration because you've done a pretty good job in those areas. Other areas will need a lot of work. This is normal. Balance in your life will come from this exercise. Think in terms of keeping each of the seven fuel tanks as full as you can."

The third principle is:

Harness the Power of Hope, Faith, and Works.

Chapter 12

Principle 4

*I count him Braver who overcomes
His desires than him who conquers
His enemies, for the hardest
Victory is over self.*
—Aristotle, BC 384-322 BC

Marilyn speaks, "Paul, your fourth principle you must learn is to:

Conquer Thyself

"Muhammad, Founder of Islam and to Islam followers, a Prophet of God, said, 'The most excellent jihad (struggle) is that for the conquest of self.'[19] He recognized man's lifelong struggle between his inner spiritual self and his carnal self. It is a story of every religion and of all mankind, the struggle of conquering one's self, to becoming rich in spirit.

"You have lived for too long at the whim of your desires. You have abandoned all discipline in your life. You have given into a life of listlessness, self-centeredness, and other self-destructive behaviors. Until you conquer yourself, you'll never return to the person you were rightly meant to be.

"It's the little foxes that destroy the vines," she continued. "You haven't murdered anyone. You didn't commit adultery while I was on earth with you. But, every day, you have been committing the little sins; deceiving others, taking from others, seeking only self-gratification, and not living life as was intended. These little daily decisions add up and eventually eat away at your life and at your potential to turn your life around. You see, the fruit on the vine eventually dies if enough of the little foxes eat away at the vine."

"So, what must I do?" I asked.

"First, forgive and humble yourself. Saint Augustine said, "Love is the beauty of the soul."[20] Until you can love yourself, it will be difficult—no, impossible—for you to live up to your potential as a human being.

"You have been hurt by others, and you have caused pain to others. You must forgive those who have caused you pain, and you must seek forgiveness for the pain you have caused others. You must be able to forgive yourself for your transgression to be able to forgive others for theirs.

"Be humble. Charles Montesquieu, 18th century French Philosopher said, 'To become truly great, one has to stand *with* people, not above them.'[21] Twentieth Century Indian philosopher, Mahatma Gandhi said, 'I claim to be a simple individual liable to err like any other fellow mortal. I own, however, that I have humility enough to confess my errors and to retrace my steps.'[22] You must begin retracing your steps. It is difficult to find peace and joy while carrying around the burdens of your and others' transgressions. Cleanse your spirit and begin anew.

"Start your day early. Achieve something toward each of your most important goals before 9:00 a.m. This begins every day with a feeling of purpose and accomplishment which is important to your overall sense you are back on the right track.

"You must work on overcoming the fears holding you back. William James told me he believed fear was the root of all that held men and women back from their full potential."

"You mean you've met William James? I remember reading about him in college. He was the one who said, 'overcome your greatest fear and the death of fear is certain.'"[23]

"Yes, Paul, he did say that. His belief was that once you realize you have control over your life you can begin experiencing life as it is meant to be. Why not pick out a fear that looms large? Overcome your greatest fear and then what can hold you back?

"Yet, introspection is necessary to determine what is holding you back. For many, the two common fears are the fear of failure and the fear of success. Those who suffer from the fear of failure won't take risks because the fear of failing is too great for them to endure. Others actually have a fear of success. To them, success will bring new burdens of responsibility they don't want. Or, maybe they may have grown up believing people of wealth only got there by 'stepping' on others. Who wants to be thought of like that?

"If it is fear of failure you suffer, know and accept that the more failure you have in your life, the closer you become to the success you dream about. Failure is an opportunity to learn important lessons and another reason for which to be grateful.

"If it is fear of success that you have, just think of all those you can bless with your success and have confidence you can grow into those responsibilities that may come. Regardless, face your fear in the eye and put it where it belongs—in your past.

"Procrastination is a common symptom of fear. Don't procrastinate. Determine each day you'll begin by doing something you've been procrastinating about and do it. You'll be surprised at how easy the rest of your day will seem."

"Paul," Sam interrupts, "I think of the words of the Nike ad, 'Just do it.' Sounds like that is Marilyn's message or what you are reporting as her message."

"You're right. And that's what I was going to do."

Marilyn continues: "Paul, nothing great was ever accomplished without *sacrifice*. You must decide what you're willing to sacrifice to have the changes in your life you want. For some, the sacrifice will be time. The education you will need to be who you want to be will take time and money. Find a way to get it done. It may be money if one is going to start a business that requires it. It may be getting off the couch and being productive toward your goals for that time of day. Replacing an hour of TV with an hour-long walk can go a long way toward helping one become fit, for example. You must recognize and determine what sacrifice you must make and are willing to make to change your life and live life abundantly. Remember what I say, nothing great has ever been accomplished without sacrifice. Are you willing to make the sacrifice?

"You've written your mission statement and if you've done that well, you should feel inspired and have a sense of *purpose* to your life. Now, live your day to evidence that. *Passion* is the evidence that what you are doing has purpose.

"When you have a growing passion, you will speak and act with *enthusiasm*. Ralph Waldo Emerson said, 'Nothing great was ever accomplished without enthusiasm.' Enthusiasm gives power to your words.

"Then, you must have the *persistence* to maintain your course despite the detractors and naysayers. I call this having pep or P.P.E.P.: *purpose, passion, enthusiasm, and persistence.* Then do all of these things with a sense of *urgency,* pep-u or *P.P.E.P.U."*

Marilyn continues, "Here's your seven-step action plan for the fourth principle:

1. *Forgive others, seek forgiveness, and forgive yourself. This will cleanse your spirit.*
2. *Decide to start each day early and achieve something right away toward your goal.*
3. *Tackle one of your greatest fears you know is holding you back. As William James said, 'Conquer your greatest fear and the death of fear is certain.'*
4. *Decide what you must sacrifice to achieve your dreams, and make the sacrifice.*
5. *Work toward your goals with a newfound purpose, passion, and enthusiasm. Enthusiasm gives power to your words and actions.*
6. *Overcome naysayers with an unwavering persistence.*
7. *Do these things with a sense of urgency.*

"These seven action steps toward conquering yourself will take you to a new level of joy and happiness. Take them to heart and change your life."

The fourth principle is:

Conquer Thyself.

Chapter 13

I don't know what your destiny will be,
But one thing I know: The only ones among you
Who will be really happy are those
Who will have sought and found how to serve others.
—Albert Schweitzer, 1875-1965
Physician, theologian, philosopher, musician,
Nobel Peace Prize recipient

"Sam, on my next visit with Marilyn, something was different. The mentor was with us as he was every day, but Marilyn was having more interaction with him. There were no spoken words; it was more like telepathically. However, when she spoke, I knew it was his words. He was more than just her mentor. I decided to name him The Master Teacher. From this moment on, I felt he was where all of this truth that Marilyn spoke originated.

"So, from these visits, I thought to myself that he was first in my mind the messenger, then the mentor, and now The Master Teacher. I liked that. I thought I would just call him TMT. You know, similar to TNT because he's so powerful. As I thought of the nickname TMT, he looked at me and held back a laugh, but smiled, knowing my thoughts as he always did."

"Paul, so much of what you have shared, though interesting, seems too magical, no offense. Don't you think most people can't become rich? That in any society only a few, maybe even less than two or three percent can become wealthy?"

"*Rich* is not what this is about. Everyone who follows these steps can be financially independent. Love, joy, and happiness can be had by all. But your statistics might be right. Remember, living life abundantly is not just about financial wealth. There are plenty of wealthy, unhappy, and dysfunctional families.

"However, from a standpoint of understanding our capitalistic system, it's not a zero sum game. A zero sum game would be similar to dividing a pie into slices where if one person gets a big slice, others must get smaller slices. That's not how capitalism works. With wealth creation, each and every American can create and attain all of the wealth his talents and ambition can provide him. I believe most Americans just don't know how to do that. These strategies can help anyone do that.

"However, here's what I've already seen in building my own business. I share these principles which I know work for everyone who'll listen. Yet, not all will follow them. The process is simple, but not easy. There's a difference. Many folks just aren't willing to set the goals and manage their daily schedules to achieve them.

"So, I suspect we'll always have those who won't succeed despite their being put on this earth to have an uncommon life. Jesus told his disciples when visiting a city that doesn't want to hear your words 'to dust off your sandals and go to the next city.'[24] It's a story as old as humankind has existed. Not everyone wants help."

"Dust off your sandals and go to the next city?"

"Sure. In other words, don't waste time with those who have closed hearts. Jesus shared a message of love, hope, forgiveness, and redemption for all. He taught a simple philosophy of loving one another as you want to be loved, of how you can live a life of joy and happiness, how you can have all of what your heart desires by serving your fellow man; yet most who heard Him and his followers turned their backs on them. There will always be those who just don't want help. If He can't influence everyone that He meets, how can I?

"Creating and building wealth is only one aspect of living life abundantly. It's not the end result that's of most import, but what we're doing for others during that process. However, in this country and many other countries, a lot of problems are solved with enough money. Financial independence should be a goal of everyone, and most problems in this country are solved with money."

"But Paul, what about the poor people who live in Ethiopia, or one of the many primitive tribes of Africa, or the Aborigines in Australia? How can some of these people who have little or no hope, many of whom will die from disease or starvation, how can this apply to them?"

"Everyone is born into this world to have a life of abundance, joy, and happiness. Don't get caught up in judging other primitive tribes by our standards. Many of them have a life of joy and abundance by their standards. If their hearts are joyful and they are serving the needs of their fellow citizens, they are being a blessing to others and they are blessed.

"But no question you're right that many are born into circumstances that seem hopeless. In countries where starvation or war takes the lives of the innocent, you can only hope their joy comes in the next life and that maybe we can improve the opportunities for their children. We are blessed to have been born into a country where our founders said in the Declaration of Independence . . . *'We hold these truths to be self-evident, that all men are created equal, that they are endowed by their Creator with certain unalienable Rights, that among these are Life, Liberty and the pursuit of Happiness.'* Liberty and capitalism can solve poverty around the world.

"Sam, let's get back to the opportunities here. Here's a story. Sam, it's a story that my father told me many years ago. He was at an insurance convention and the speaker was the leading sales person for a large insurance company. He came to America as an immigrant with not a penny to his name. Although he could not speak English and had nothing, he became a great life insurance salesman and became wealthy. He said to the group of salespeople as he stood at the podium: 'Many Americans made fun of me when I told them I came to America because I grew up being told in America, the streets are paved in gold. The fact is . . . they are and most of you don't see that.'"

"Paul, that's interesting, isn't it?"

"Yes, but let me repeat. All of what I'm being taught is not about how I can be wealthy and buy all of the things I want. A life lived to accumulate things is not a fulfilling life. Yet, a life lived to serve and help others achieve their dreams will come back to benefit us. It's almost like saying it's selfish to live selflessly. But if your heart simply wants things, you're living selfishly, and that's not the same thing."

"Paul, I've noticed that the happiest people I've met are people who are actively involved in organizations helping others. It's their service to others that seems to give meaning to their lives. Is that the basic principle here?"

"Yes. Mihaly Csikszentmihalyi—try saying that three times or even once—says, 'life becomes serene and enjoyable precisely when selfish pleasure and personal success are no longer the guiding goals.'"[25]

"Is he someone Marilyn has met in the spirit world? Incredible! You have me asking such a question! I am definitely suspending my belief aren't I?"

"To answer your first question, no, he's still alive. He's just a smart guy. To answer your second question, yes, you haven't rolled your eyes once today."

That draws a laugh from Sam.

Chapter 14

Principle 5

The high destiny of the individual is to serve rather than to rule.
—Albert Einstein, 1879-1955
Noted mathematician, physicist, philosopher,
Nobel Peace Prize recipient,
Developed law of relativity.

Marilyn speaks, "The fifth principle is:

Uncommon Success Always Includes Serving Others."

"Sam, when I share with you what I do with the homeless, how I teach others to reach their dreams, I am living this fifth important principle. Marilyn told me a story that if you scatter seeds upon the ground, then night and day, whether you are asleep or are awake, those seeds would sprout and grow. You may not understand how that works, but if you will sow those seeds, you'll harvest many times more than the seeds you planted.[26] She said this was as natural a law as gravity. And even as gravity is only now being understood, the law of sowing and reaping needn't be understood by you to be enjoyed by you. Sow your seeds and live abundantly.

"Here is what I've learned: When sowing seeds, we know some will fall upon ground that is not fertile. But that is as expected. The place where the seeds take hold and grow will return riches many thousands of times more than what you sowed. But I didn't understand how this was to work for me."

Then she said: "The seeds you sow are the lives you affect positively. Share yourself with others in positive ways, and it'll come back to benefit you many times. Your goal is to discover how you can serve others. The more you are able to positively serve others, the more rewards you will experience. Rewards come in many forms including spiritual, emotional, and financial."

Marilyn continues: "Serving others also means living life as a cheerful giver.[27] Giving is about doing for others without any expectation for return. It is this property that makes the act of giving so powerful.

"Giving can take many forms. You can give of your time, your talents, and your money. Your time is the most precious commodity you have in this life. You don't know how much time you have, but you know each minute that passes is that much less time you have left. To give of your time to help someone or help a worthwhile organization is a great sacrifice and will be rewarded.

"Remember, serving others and giving to others in need is the evidence that you are acting with love in your heart. Og Mandino said, 'Do all things with love.'[28] Love is the fabric of a purposeful and passionate life."

"Marilyn, you have met Og Mandino? I read a few of his books, 'The Greatest Salesman in the World,' 'The Gift of Acabar,' and 'The Christ Commission' among them. And you met him?"

"No, I just heard he said that." Marilyn quipped.

Sam interrupts with this example: "Paul, I knew a lady; her name was Alma, and she spent many hours and days of her life giving to families she never knew. In fact, it could be said she did work for the dead. Her faith believed that recording the birth and death records for the deceased was an important mission in life. So she visited cemeteries every weekend, spending from dawn until dusk, and recorded the information from the tombstones which would then be taken to and recorded at state libraries for families to trace their ancestors. She did this tirelessly for most all of her adult life."[29] Paul, this would be a great example of serving others, but also of works being the evidence of your faith, wouldn't it?"

"Yes. Absolutely! Imagine the faith required to continue such difficult and generally thankless work for a lifetime. Giving your time, money to your church, to your charity, to a relative or friend who is in need, these are gifts from which you will be rewarded if given with no expectation of reward. Such gifts should be made with a cheerful heart."

"Paul, can I stop you here for a moment? When the wealthy give donations to their church, aren't they simply trying to 'buy' their way into the graces of God? Isn't there even a Bible verse that says something about 'it is easier for a camel to fit through the eye of a needle than a rich man to enter into heaven'?"[30]

"If you seek riches so you can have precious things, you'll not enjoy a life of abundance as I was being taught. But if you seek to serve your fellow human beings in a spirit of love, then your riches will be beyond what you can imagine. Remember, nearly every person in the Old and New Testaments who were 'men of God' were blessed with wealth and riches. Even the twelve disciples who gave up everything to follow Jesus to spread His gospel did not want for anything. Loving God and serving your fellow man always brought a life of abundance to believers.[31]

"In the Old Testament, the son of David was Solomon. Solomon became king and served his people with compassion, humility and with obedience to God. You've heard of the 'Wisdom of Solomon?'"

"Yes," Sam says.

"His heart was pure. He became the wealthiest king in all the land. He did not ask for wealth. He became wealthy because his heart was pure, and he was blessed with riches. The Bible is filled with stories of men who served their fellow men and were blessed with riches and lived lives of abundance.

"It's all about what is in your heart. An unrighteous man cannot buy righteousness. It is said you cannot serve two masters. Money as your master, accumulating money and doing nothing for others is a negative kind of wealth and is what we must guard against. When we're warned that you cannot serve two masters for you will love one and despise the other, this is what is meant. But sharing your good fortune without expectation of reward is a blessing to both the recipient and to the donor, no question about that. What we give to others without expectation of return will come back to benefit us many times over. Harness the power of serving others and giving without expectation and watch your life grow in richness."

"The world would be a better place if everyone practiced that."

"You're right. Sam, I knew I wanted to build a business serving others the best way I was able. The law that Marilyn was describing to me says if I serve others, then I'll be richly rewarded provided my heart and my desires are to help others attain their dreams. I wanted to do just that.

"My action plan for this was simple: First, I wanted to find a business that helped others. Second, I wanted to do something for someone every day that had nothing to do with my business and came with no expectation. Finally, I wanted to share a portion of my income with a charity I could enthusiastically support. With these three activities combined, I knew I would be a great blessing to many and to me. It excited me!"

"The fifth principle is:

Uncommon Success Always Includes Serving Others.

Chapter 15

Principle 6

To be happy is easy enough if we give ourselves,
Forgive others, and live with thanksgiving.
No self-centered person,
No ungrateful soul can ever be happy,
Much less make anyone else happy.
Life is giving, not getting.
—Joseph Fort Newton, 1876-1950
Mason, Minister, philosopher, author

Marilyn speaks: "Paul, you've lost your capacity to be thankful because you don't recognize why you should be thankful. You have grown bitter. You have drifted far from the person you were meant to be. Your sixth principle is simple:

Live a Life of Gratitude.

"Your life is made up of your experiences. The knowledge you have gained is because of those experiences, and you should be thankful for them. Even when you are going through difficult times, you must be thankful. You must learn to live a life of gratitude.

"Paul, Cicero said, 'gratitude is not only the greatest of virtues, but the mother of all the rest.'"[32]

"Marilyn," I said to her, "You're actually getting to meet these great thinkers from the world's history and sit down and speak to them just as we are now? That is just too cool."

"Yes, that's how it works here, and you're getting to learn from them as well. So, Paul, I want you to make a list of all of those things for which you are grateful, and I want you to review that list often. But I want you to do something else. List all of the things you believe were curses in your life: life's tragedies, mistakes others made that hurt you, decisions you made that hurt you or others. I want you to find a way to be thankful for something about those occurrences."

"Why?" I asked.

"I want you to begin a process of living a life of gratitude and of humility. Humility comes from humbling yourself—accepting your human nature. Accepting your mistakes and learning from your mistakes will help you grow and make your life fuller.

"Remember, don't be the judge of what is and what isn't a blessing. Be thankful in everything. You are nilpotent; God is omnipotent. That's why you must be thankful for all things because you are unable to judge what is and what isn't a blessing."

"I did what she asked. I made a list of all of my blessings and discovered there was much more to be thankful for than I'd realized. I listed those many tragedies, setbacks and mistakes I experienced and I made. I looked for ways to see how they also were in some ways blessings. I had to admit to myself the lies and the pain I caused others and to myself. It was cathartic. The darkness that had grown to envelop my life began to disappear. Even my journey from a wonderful life with the girl of my dreams to a life of despair, street begging and homelessness was beginning to look like there were reasons to be thankful."

"How so?" Sam asked.

"I learned and grew from my new understanding I was able to survive even without any of the necessities most of us take for granted: a home, a car, the security of a safe place to rest, knowing from where your next meal will come. I survived without any of that. That was a blessing.

"I know how to be poor and I lived through it. I know both circumstances—that is, times of prosperity and times of suffering. I have the wisdom that comes from experiencing both." I am ready to learn how to live a life of abundance." So the sixth principle is:

Live a Life of Gratitude

Chapter 16

Principle 7

I dread success. To have succeeded is to have finished one's business on earth,
Like the male spider, who is killed by the female the moment he has
Succeeded in courtship. I like a state of continual becoming,
With a goal in front and not behind.
—George Bernard Shaw, 1856-1950
Co-founder of London School of Economics,
Playwright, Nobel Peace Prize recipient

"I have no idea in real time how long all of this took to implant in my brain, but it was coming to an end, as I was now ready for the seventh and final principle."

Marilyn speaks:" "Paul, are you ready for your final principle?"

"Yes."

She continues, "This last one seems so obvious, yet so many people believe once they have reached some age such as: 30, 40, 50, 60, 70 or whatever age that they cannot change their lives, and that is just not true. The seventh principle is:

It is Never Too Late to Attain Your Dreams . . . Never."

"Sam, you have heard the old axiom, 'you can't teach an old dog new tricks.' Well, the fact is—you can teach an old dog new tricks . . . provided the old dog wants to learn new tricks.

"I know of a factory worker whose name was Earl who was married and had a child. While in his thirties, he decided he wanted more for his family. He went back to school and got his degree in Pre-Med and was able to get accepted into medical school and sure enough, he became a family physician at the age of forty-one. He did not accept there was an age limit for achieving his dreams."

Sam says, "Paul, one of my heroes is an Olympic swimmer whose name is Dara Torres. Dara first appeared in the 1984 Olympics. She has been in five Olympics winning twelve medals in all, including four gold medals, in a sport usually reserved for very young athletes. In the 2008 Olympics at age 41, she competed in three events and won silver medals in each of them. Most impressive, a year earlier at age 40 in 2007, fifteen months after giving birth, she broke her own American record in the 50-meter freestyle, twenty-six years after she first set the American record at age fifteen.[33] She was unwilling to let age define her and became the fastest woman in America while old enough to be every other competitor's mother. You're right; it's never too late to be what you want."

"Sam, that is a great example of what I'm talking about. Here's an example of how one can achieve uncommon success even later in life. We talked about McDonald's. Ray Kroc was its founder. For most of his life, he had tried a number of different trades with little success. He actually worked for room and board at a restaurant just to learn the business.

"A few years later, he became a milkshake mixer salesman, and that's how he met the McDonald brothers—two brothers who, together, owned ten restaurants. Those restaurants were built similar to the shape and size of a tennis court. The brothers had purchased milkshake mixers from Ray Kroc for each of their ten stores. Ray believed he could take their idea—their style of hamburger restaurant—nationally and in 1961 at the age of 59, he purchased the stores and the rights to what we know as McDonald's, and he built the most successful restaurant chain in history."[34]

"So success can happen at any age if you employ the principles; is that what you are saying?"

"Yes. I know so."

"Paul, I'll share a success story with you about a woman who lived for years in my home state of New York. It speaks to the idea that you are describing. It is about Anna Mary Robertson who grew up on a farm in Virginia and had almost no formal education. She lived on a farm most of her life having married a farm worker and was a hardworking woman supporting her husband. They moved to New York where they worked a farm until his death.

"She began doing embroidery for hire until arthritis prevented her from doing so at age seventy-six. She found that, even with her arthritis, she could paint, and so she taught herself to paint. She began to sell her paintings at age seventy-eight for two dollars if it was on a small canvas and three dollars if it was on a large canvas. She painted a total of thirty-six hundred canvases.

"When an art promoter saw her paintings in a drug store in her local community, he arranged for a showing. She soon became famous and the prices of her work skyrocketed. Today, she is best known by most as Grandma Moses, one of the greatest American painters in history."

"Grandma Moses . . . she definitely illustrates that it is never too late," Paul says.

"Sam, let me get back to Marilyn's message to me."

Marilyn speaks to Paul: "There was a story of a wealthy rancher who hired most all who came to his ranch looking for work. Those who arrived early would be paid ten dollars for a days' work. But it was noticed by some of the workers that the same ten-dollar wage was paid to those who came at the end of the day.

"One worker asked the owner: 'Why? Why should they who worked only at the end of the day receive the same wage as those who worked all day?' The land owner asked: 'Are those who come to find their way late lesser than those who found their way early? Isn't it never too late to find ones way?'

"Paul," Marilyn continues, "many of the people you will come into contact with will already have lost their way and many will already have been downtrodden by life's difficulties. Your passion and enthusiasm will be needed to give hope to those who believe they have no hope. But you will have that gift as you live these principles. Share with them what you have learned, and you will change the lives of all of those who have open hearts and hear your truth."

"So, Sam, I was beginning to feel I had a mission in life, and I was beginning to understand. I did not know what I was going to do or how I was going to do it, but I was beginning to get the picture."

Chapter 17

In Summary

"Sam, let me summarize the seven life lessons I learned from Marilyn:

1. *Realize that you must first believe you have those things you want before you have those things, and then you will have them.* The prayer or meditation you create speaks to this.
2. *Know that changing your words can change your life.* You begin this with a new mission statement for your life, and you speak that often. You also become aware of what you say and recognize you are speaking toward or away from your life dreams.
3. *Harness the power of hope, faith, and works.* Writing down your hopes and dreams begins the process of making them concrete goals. You categorize them as to the seven areas or 'fuel tanks' of your life that you need to nourish or fill. You organize them as to a time table for accomplishment and as to their importance to you. You include details of those dreams so you can visualize them and make them real in your mind's eye. You do the work necessary toward realizing those goals. That work is the daily evidence of your faith that your goal will be achieved.
4. Now the real work begins. Here's your seven-step action plan for the fourth principle, *'Conquer Thyself,'* or taking control of you.

   - Decide to start each day early and achieve something right away toward your goal.
   - Tackle one of your greatest fears you know is holding you back. As William James said, 'Conquer your greatest fear and the death of fear is certain.'

- Decide what you must sacrifice to achieve your dreams and make the sacrifice.
- Work toward your goals with a newfound purpose. Purpose gives way to passion and passion is the evidence what you are doing is important. Put power in your message with enthusiasm.
- Overcome naysayers with an unwavering persistence.
- Do these things with a sense of urgency.

5. *Uncommon success always includes serving others.* My action plan for this was simple. First, I wanted to find a business that helped others. Second, I wanted to do something for someone every day that had nothing to do with my business and came with no expectation. Finally, I wanted to share a portion of my income with a charity I could enthusiastically support. With these three activities combined, I knew I'd be a great blessing to many and to me. It excited me!

6. *Live a life of gratitude.* That means finding your way of being grateful *for* everything and *in* everything. Don't judge. Be thankful.

7. *Know that it's never too late to attain your dreams . . . never.* Don't give up on your life of uncommon success. Don't ever give up."

Chapter 18

Surprise!

"Sam, it's been a good day. Will you excuse me for a moment?"

"Sure"

Sam thinking to herself: The time has flown by today. I haven't even gotten to take the photos I need. At this point in the day, I know the light won't be good, so I'll stay another day to finish up. I don't believe my editor, Vince, is going to be too impressed. This story isn't for our magazine. I'm hoping to get Paul to make an exception and let me photograph the flowers in the secret garden. That would get the article published, I'm convinced.

As I stretch and walk from the sitting room, through the foyer and toward the entrance to the house, I look out the large entry window facing the circular driveway that goes around the fountain and to the entrance, and I notice a vehicle has arrived. From the back door of the SUV pop two small children, a girl and a boy. They seem to be around five to six years old. The driver is a beautiful woman in her thirties. Paul startles me from behind.

"Well, Sam, I guess we're done for the day, huh?"

"I think so. I would like to stop by tomorrow and take those photographs we discussed. By the way, Paul, about that secret garden . . ." I'm interrupted by the sounds of two excited children running full force into the room.

"Daddy, daddy, daddy!" screamed the little girl, the taller of the two, followed closely by whom I presume to be her little brother.

Sam in shock thinking to herself: How could this be? I didn't even know he had children and surely he would've mentioned to me if he had a wife. I know Marilyn died before they had children because they were saving for their first home while living, just the two of them, in the apartment.

Paul hugs and kisses each enthusiastically as if he had not seen them for a long time. "Sam, I want you to meet my daughter, Katelyn, and my son, Luke. Kids, this is Miss Samantha Hodges."

"Hello Miss Hodges," says Katelyn.

"Hi" says Luke.

"How do you do?" Following the children into the room was, now, an obviously very beautiful woman, with an elegance, dignity, and charm about her. The warmth of her smile was radiant. She is the kind of woman who would garner everyone's attention when entering a crowded room. Paul kisses her and warmly hugs her.

Turning to me, he says, "Sam, I want to introduce you to my wife, the love of my life . . . Marilyn."

My jaw drops!

Chapter 19

I am stunned. Why have I been listening to this made-up story about how his wife—this picture of perfection standing before me—had died? For two days, I've taken copious notes about his life events, how Marilyn had died, how his dad had died, then he lost his mother, he went off the deep end, begged for food, and then he was hit by a drunk driver similar to the kind of accident that supposedly killed Marilyn. Did any of these stories even happen? I mean, did Paul even get hit by a vehicle? Obviously, Marilyn did not. What were the past two days about?

Paul said he learned from Marilyn while he visited her in the spirit world. How foolish was I to even entertain his delusions. I have no idea now what is true and what isn't. I'm getting madder by the second. I have nothing that my editor will print. I've been here for two days, have no photos and this whole story that has kept me here, interested, is bogus. It's all I can do to remain poised and calm. But, I'll try.

With a seething anger: "Marilyn, how interesting it is to meet you. I'm Samantha Hodges of 'The Life Styles of the Rich Magazine.' I don't know what to say right now. I'm a reporter lost for words."

"It's great to meet you. Sounds like you may have learned some things from Paul, I'm guessing? Judging from your face, I'm betting Paul has been telling you his story. Anyway, you've met Katelyn and Luke I can see. Kids, go help Debbie bring in your things."

"Well Sam, I'm sure you're pretty confused," Paul says. "Marilyn, honey, I was telling my story the last couple of days to Sam and your showing up has probably created some questions on Sam's part."

"That may be a gross understatement if ever there was one," Sam says sarcastically.

"Samantha, you look like you need to sit down. If you don't mind, I'd like to go get unpacked and, maybe, take a shower. I very much want to talk with you, Samantha, but I'm exhausted. Please forgive me. Are you going to be here tomorrow?"

"I think so. I mean, I need to get some photographs, and I just don't know what to think right now."

"Maybe Paul can put you to ease, but I would like to see you tomorrow before you leave. It was nice meeting you, Samantha."

"You too, I think . . . I mean . . . I've never met a ghost before. I'm sorry."

Paul speaks. "Well, Sam, we probably have some more talking to do, huh?"

"It is taking all my restraint not to rip up all of my notes and head back right now. I've never been treated like this. You just choose to make up a good story to lay on a New York reporter for fun? Why?"

"Sam, I know this will be hard for you to accept, but what I told you is true."

"Then something is wrong with you, Paul. Marilyn is quite obviously alive and well. Spirit world? You aren't well, Paul, if you can stand there and tell me what you told to me is true."

"Don't judge me right now. There is a reason I was encouraged to tell you what I did; something I have never shared with anyone, except Marilyn, and I think there is a reason for me to complete this story with you. I didn't believe I would ever share this with anyone . . . at least, anyone except Marilyn. I want you to relax, don't throw anything away just yet, and come back in the morning and spend some time with Marilyn. Would you do that?"

"I think I have to. I may not have a job to go back to, but I'll see you tomorrow."

Chapter 20

After showering, Marilyn joins Paul in the sitting room.

Paul speaks: "I missed you. A week without you and the kids seemed like a month. How were your mother and father?"

"They were well and just couldn't get over how much Katelyn and Luke have grown since our last visit. Katelyn sang songs to them, and they just thought she sounded like an angel. Luke took the TV remote and reprogrammed it. You know Luke. He can figure out anything electronic.

"The drive didn't seem that bad this time. I guess I'm getting used to it. Only took about six hours to get home. But, I'm tired.

"Samantha seems like a sharp person, but she didn't seem too pleased to meet me."

"I didn't prepare her for your arrival. I didn't think you would be here before she left today. I'm hoping you can talk to her tomorrow. I don't know, maybe it's just too fantastic for anyone to believe."

"How much have you shared with her?"

"I told her how I learned the seven secrets. I told her about your death, my visit to you in the spirit world, and the lessons you taught me while being watched over by The Master Teacher. That's it."

"That had to go over well when I walked in. I'm surprised you told her that much."

"Well, I didn't intend to. It just sort of came out over the time together. She has been here two days."

"It has never come out with anyone else. Again, I'm just surprised you told someone you don't know who is in a position to share whatever she wants with the whole world. Paul, do you plan to share everything with her?"

"I don't know. If I don't, she'll think I've made up all of this. If I do, she'll surely think I'm nuts and belong in a hospital. So which do I prefer she believe? I just don't know."

"Do you want my opinion?"

"Yes."

"She's a reporter, right? You've just met her. You've not shared any of this with anyone, family or friends, and she's neither."

"What do you suggest?"

"Let me tell her what happened from my point of view. She will begin to see why you think what you do and perhaps not conclude you are either a liar or nuts."

"But you know I'm not a liar, and I'm not nuts. I wish I could just go back to the idea to tell her I was homeless and won the lottery. That's what I should've done."

"I'll meet with her tomorrow and try to undo what you've done. Now, I really want to get some rest."

Chapter 21

"Vince, Sam."

"Hello, Sam. Where are you? Are you back here in New York?"

"No. I'll be here in Montana one more day, and then I'll be on my way back."

"I'm not happy about this. I'm not hearing anything in your voice that tells me this trip was worth the time or money. Do you have us a story?"

"You're breaking up. Hello . . . Hello . . . I'll call you when I get back."

Chapter 22

The Final Day

Sam has packed her bags and is prepared for her trip. Almost magically, Pedro taps on her door to offer his help in taking her bags to the driver who waits to take Sam back to Paul's home for her final visit. As Pedro retrieves her bags and runs ahead of her, she pauses, digs into her purse and pulls out a twenty-dollar bill to leave on the bed as a tip. She thought of her visit, the service, the warm surroundings, and the plentiful plate of food brought to her each day. So she reaches back into her purse and pulls out an additional four twenty-dollar bills to leave a generous hundred-dollar tip on the bed. She heads for Paul's home.

"Good morning, Sam!" Paul greets her at the entrance to his home.

"Good morning? I'm not sure. I gave very serious consideration to going back to the airport instead of coming here, Paul."

"Well, Sam, I'm glad you came by. I've asked Marilyn to visit with you this morning. I hope you'll enjoy your visit, and I'm sure you'll have plenty of questions. Don't give up on me yet. I've never gone through this with anyone except Marilyn—the person you're visiting with this morning. She should be down in a minute. While you wait, help yourself to the fruit tray Debbie has prepared for you. I'm going to visit with Krista, one of my distributors.

"Thank you."

Chapter 23

Marilyn enters the den where Sam is snacking on the fruit. Marilyn's warm smile disarms Sam and creates a relaxed environment.

"Good morning, Samantha."

"Good morning to you, Marilyn. You can't imagine how surprised I was to see you."

"I bet. I'm sure you have some questions."

"For sure. Please, call me Sam. Everyone does."

"So, Sam, where would you like to begin?"

"Marilyn, how can Paul tell such a story when you are standing here in front of me, obviously, alive and well? Unless you are not the same Marilyn who was killed in a car accident. I just don't know what is and what isn't true from the two days I spent with Paul, meaning no offense to either of you. I'm just puzzled by all of this."

"Sam, I understand, I know. But you have spent a couple of days with Paul, right?"

"Yes."

"Does Paul strike you as a person who would lie to you?"

"I did not think so until you walked in. But no, he doesn't seem like such a person."

"Okay Sam, let me see if I can shed some light on this. You may have to be a little forgiving of Paul's story which, by the way, he believes to be true. However, I think you'll find what I have to say to be easier to understand.

"Sam, did Paul tell you about coming home from work the day I was killed by the drunk driver?"

"Yes. But do you understand—or should I say hear—what you are saying? Pretty ridiculous, don't you think?"

"Yes, but bear with me. What exactly did he say?"

"Let me see if I can find that in my notes. He said: 'Suddenly, I felt like I was hit by a truck. I knew something was wrong.' Or something like that. He was afraid he'd never see you again and when he got back to your apartment, the police were there to tell him you had been hit by a drunk driver."

"So, he said he felt like he had been hit by a truck?"

"Yes."

"You see Sam, Paul was hit by a truck. Did he tell you he had an eerie feeling and he felt like his heart was pounding?"

"Yes."

"His heart was pounding . . . his eerie feeling? . . . it was at that moment he was critically injured and was to end up going into a coma for more than eight months. You see, I was not struck; he was. Everything he described to you after that very real event was what he imagined while in his life-threatening state from that accident."

"So, you were never in an accident . . . just him."

"Correct. Did he tell you he lost everything, including his parents, became homeless, and was struck by another drunk driver like the one who struck me?"

"Yes. He said all of those things. So, he actually just dreamed those things while in his coma that resulted from *his* accident, not yours? So, he obviously never visited you in the spirit world because you were never the one who had died. He dreamed all of that. He tells his story as if it were true. I began to almost believe it, silly me.

"There was never a messenger, or mentor . . . wait a minute, The Master Teacher I believe he called him. Yes! TMT who, through you, revealed the 'truth.' All of this newfound knowledge he learned in the spirit world never happened, but was just him dreaming. Is that the truth?"

"Oh, it happened, just not like he described. You see, for those eight months he was in the coma, I read to him every day from great works he always wanted to read, but could never find the time. I read to him from the works of Aristotle, Plato, and Socrates. I read to him essays and poetry from Emerson, the biographies of such great entrepreneurs as Carnegie, Ray Kroc, Sam Walton and others. About Lincoln, Jefferson, and JFK. But, most of all, I read to him from the Bible because I felt that was the Book we needed the most if we were going to get through this tragedy.

"I was assured he'd never come out of the coma and, if he did, I probably would wish he hadn't. When he did come out of the coma, they said he would never be normal, and he would certainly never walk again.

"Yet, he was different. All of those months of hearing nothing but great works, positive words, the truths of life, and how to live this life most definitely got through to him. It is the only explanation that makes sense. When he came out from his coma, he had a glow unlike ever before. He knew he would get all of his abilities back, and he knew he was destined to make a difference. You could just feel it. It was something!"

"But, why does he stick with this story of his which is so obviously a tale? He knows you didn't die, and you didn't teach him from the spirit world. What you are saying is still such a wonderful and fantastic story. It certainly does not need to be made into something it isn't."

"I'm not sure I can answer that for you, Sam. But what I've told you is what happened, and I hope you can be kind with any reporting you do about this."

"Marilyn, I don't believe you have anything to worry about. Vince, my editor, isn't interested in such a story. He wants a simple twelve-paragraph piece about rags to riches, helping the homeless, and here are the photos of an opulent home and lifestyle. That's all. I'm not sure we have that. But, you could help me with an important detail which could help me a great deal with Vince."

"How?"

"Debbie showed me the 'secret garden' and specifically, the flower garden. The unique beauty and brilliance of those flowers is extraordinary. If I could get some pictures of that flower garden, I believe I could save the story, get it published, and take some heat off of me for all of the time I've taken here."

"I'm sorry, Sam, but that's just not possible. Paul has such a strong feeling about that place. You were blessed to be taken there. That says something about you. But, he wants you to keep that moment in your memory only. He forbids any photographs to be taken of it. I'm sorry."

"That's what Debbie said, also. Is there any chance Paul might make an exception, given my predicament?"

"He's an opened-minded person, and he'll not be offended by your asking."

"Well Marilyn, I so enjoyed speaking with you. You have made all of this clearer."

"Paul should be back by lunch time. Why don't you take any photos you want to take. I'll make us some lunch, and you can have a few minutes with Paul before you leave. Does that work for you?"

"It does. Thanks."

Chapter 24

"Thanks for lunch. That was delicious. Marilyn, that salad was terrific. I'd love to have the recipe for your dressing. I could taste the garlic, the feta cheese, olive oil, maybe a little white wine vinegar?"

"Marilyn's secret recipe," says Paul. "She'll die with it."

"No, I won't. Sam, I'll copy it for you. Before you leave, I'll have the recipe for you to take with you. I'm glad you enjoyed it."

"Sam," says Paul, "Why don't you and I take a little walk; you can get any other questions you have for me answered, and we'll get you back toward the airport. Is that fair?"

"Great."

Together, they walk through his home and onto the patio. "Paul, you have a beautiful home and an interesting story. No doubt, interesting."

"Thank you, Sam. But are you trying to ask me something? Was Marilyn's description of what happened easier for you to understand?"

"Yes, for sure. I guess I'm puzzled why you told me what you did. I mean, you could've said what you told me seemed to be true, it just wasn't. Marilyn, obviously, did not die, and you couldn't have visited her in the spirit world.

"I mean, while in a coma, just the fact you learned all of those concepts and lessons while being read to by Marilyn is extraordinary. Contrary to what science believes, your life changed from what Marilyn read to you while in a coma. Imagine that! You survived in the face of what doctors said was hopeless. Doctors don't believe that a person is capable of learning anything while in a comatose state. You did. That's fantastic enough. Isn't it?"

We're at the final moment. She's begging for an explanation. I was hoping this moment would never come, but I knew it would. For years, I've shared this with no one, except Marilyn. Marilyn did her best to give her the explanation that would be the easiest to believe. It was the truth from Marilyn's point of view for years. Yet, Marilyn knows that what she shared with Sam does not explain everything. On the surface, what Marilyn told her seems to be the logical explanation. But, do I share with this person whom I barely know the most intimate and important additional fact to this story? I decide . . . I just can't.

"Sam, there are moments that are so powerful in your life you cannot accept what seems like a logical explanation when the facts as you see them point to something else. I know Marilyn is alive, and it seems that she taught me from my bedside. I guess I know that. But, to me, I lived her death, the death of each of my parents, and my near death. I visited her in the spirit world, and that seems so real to me, that's the only way I can describe it. I can't explain it any better. I know I may seem delusional in this matter, but that's what the truth is to me."

"Okay, Paul. Then I just have one more favor to ask before I go. The only way I'm going to get your story published and keep me out of hot water is to get a couple of photos of your secret garden, particularly the flower garden. Marilyn thought, or maybe I thought, you might make an exception to your rule if I appealed to your kindness and asked for your help. I may lose my job over the time and money I've spent here without a story to publish. Those flowers will guarantee the story will get published. How about it? Can you make an exception for me?"

I know that my answer is "no" and that is final. But, since my near-death experience, visiting the spirit world, and learning the seven secrets to living life abundantly, I've worked very hard at living my life inspiring, uplifting, and being honest with those I meet. I certainly don't want to jeopardize Sam's job. If I say "no" with no explanation, Sam will leave not believing I live the way I've been speaking. If I tell her the rest of what happened, she may think I'm nuts. It seems that this moment remains stubbornly here for a reason. After a long and silent moment . . .

Chapter 25

"Sam, come with me."

I lead Sam back into the house through the foyer, past the living room, past the large sitting room where we have spent some of our time together and back toward the den, or library. I ask Sam to wait at the door, while I prepare for the rest of this story. I go to my desk in the den and from the center drawer, I remove two brass keys.

I go to the book shelves on the east wall of the library and remove a very large, heavy dictionary that's hiding a small button. Upon pushing the button, a portion of the wall with book-laden shelves moves slowly away from the remainder of the east wall to reveal a small room behind it. When the moving wall completes its rotation, it becomes flush with the south wall of the hidden room. The walls, floor, and ceiling of the room are made from a beautiful black walnut. The room is twelve-by-twelve feet and is anchored in the middle by an ornately carved cabinet made from a deep, rich cherry wood. The room is softly lit with four wall lamps made from antique, brass candelabras. I ask Sam to join me.

I take one of the brass keys and slip it into the lock on the large double doors of the cabinet. Inside the doors are three drawers, and I slide open the middle drawer. From the drawer, I remove a locked mahogany box, similar in size to a cigar box. Carefully, I take the box to the left, or west, wall of the room, where there is a stand designed for the box to sit upon. I use the second key to unlock the mahogany box. This is the first time this room has been visited by anyone except Marilyn and me.

The contractor who built my home was instructed to leave this space behind the library unfinished. He had no idea what I had in mind for the space. Then, I had the room completed by a very special craftsman and friend. The secret nature and the sacred nature of this room were understood by him, but not why or what the contents would be.

I could tell Sam understood the importance of this moment. She knew she was about to learn something that was significant to me. What I knew was—her reality would change forever.

Having unlocked the box, I lifted the lid and revealed an envelope. I moved to my right so Sam could see the envelope.

Sam speaks softly, but with excitement she could not contain. "This is amazing. It is like nothing I have ever seen. What material is it made of? The brightness is breathtaking. I just have never seen anything like it!"

The envelope is a brilliant white, yet, simultaneously, gold-like. It is so beautiful beyond description, so hard to describe. I carefully pick up the envelope. I open it and remove a letter that appears to be made of the same unique material. The letter is perfect in every way except for a tear in the bottom left corner where a piece has been removed. The letter appeared to be hand-written, but was without flaw. I hand the letter to Sam and ask her to read it aloud.

Chapter 26

Sam reads the letter.

Dear Paul,

You now have all of the knowledge to serve others and to live life abundantly. I have enclosed in this envelope a handful of seeds. These seeds are like none other. Sprinkle them on the ground in a very special place, and they will multiply ten thousand fold. Their beauty will reward you ten thousand fold provided that you take the seeds of wisdom you now have in your newfound knowledge, and spread them to others, teaching them how they can also plant their own seeds and be rewarded ten thousand fold. As long as you continue on your path and live by the truth you have learned, serving others and helping others reach their goals, your rewards will multiply ten thousand fold, and you will have all of the love and happiness you can imagine. Serve others with humility and good cheer and you will be exalted.

Share your gifts with those who are open to them and want to change their lives. These flowers will grow in any climate, in any soil, in any place where there is love and nurturing. They are not to be exploited or used to benefit anyone except the persons you feel are ready for their magic.

Be warned. You will come to have challengers and detractors. There are always naysayers and critics on the sideline, and you will have them aplenty. Be not afraid. Dust off your shoes and go to where there are those eager to learn what you have to teach, and teach them how to sprinkle their own seeds upon the ground.

Yours truly,

TMT

Sam pauses, taking all of what she is seeing into her mind, not yet able to calculate the meaning or significance of such a remarkable document . . . until her eyes drop to the bottom of the page. What she now reads will change her perception of miracles and will change her life forever. It will challenge everything she ever believed before this moment.

Chapter 27

Beneath the signature Sam reads this post script:

I have arranged for Marilyn to return to the physical world with you to be your companion. The two of you will live a long and abundant life together having children, grandchildren, and great-grandchildren, all of whom will be a blessing to you and will be blessed by you. You will be a great blessing to your community and to society as you sprinkle your seeds across the ground.

Chapter 28

After gazing upon the letter and what it might mean for some minutes, Sam returns it to me. I carefully return it to its envelope, placing it back in the box, into the drawer, and closing the double doors of the cabinet where it will stay. I seal the room and quietly leave the den and return to the sitting area.

Sam asks, "How did you come by this letter?"

"The moment I awakened from my coma, it was sitting on my bed near my right arm. Understand, I never uttered a word throughout my eight months in this coma. I only thought of the personage who was with us throughout as The Master Teacher and, in my mind, nicknamed him TMT.

"But I read the letter and knew it was true. I knew Marilyn would be there with me although she had died years before. I knew this. Can you see why I can't just tell the story as Marilyn understands it? Her explanation makes sense. But I know mine is real.

"As I read the letter for the first time, I knew I needed to protect it and keep this to myself. Before anyone knew I had awakened from my coma, I hid the letter beneath my mattress. It stayed there until I was able to move, and able to locate a safer place for it in the room. I didn't even say a word about it to Marilyn.

"When I first saw Marilyn come into the room, I was moved to tears of joy and happiness. She was also, but she had no idea what I had been through, and she had no memory of being with me in the spirit world. She—as did everyone except me—believed the accident was only to me and she was here and taught me all of those things from my bed side. That was everyone's reality except mine.

"As my strength grew, and I became mobile, I tore a piece from the letter and took it to Brigham Young University where they have sophisticated technology to determine the molecular structure and the origin of unknown substances. The conclusion drawn from testing the letter's fabric was that it was of no known substance anywhere on Earth. I know there are no other flowers on the planet like the ones you have seen whose seeds came from this envelope—delivered to me by no one who was ever seen, or ever known to have come into my room.

"It took me more than four years to share this letter with Marilyn. It wasn't until we built this house and she was puzzled by the secret room that two different builders participated in creating that I told her about it. Until now, she was the only one who knew the entire story. Even Marilyn does not know what to think about it all."

This turn of events was weighing heavily upon Sam. She was in a pensive state when Marilyn entered and called to us.

"Hi Sam, Paul. I have the recipe copied for you. How was your visit?"

"I think Sam is still a little speechless, Marilyn."

"Yes, I guess I am. I came here for a story, and I'm leaving with so many questions that may never be answered. Life seems to be taking on more meaning than I ever imagined and I . . ."

"You visited the, uh . . ."

"Yes, Marilyn. I took Sam into the 'room.' She has seen everything."

Marilyn says: "Sam, I'm not sure you will ever figure out everything you've learned here. I haven't and Paul even questions the fantastic nature of it all. But what I've come to know is that those simple principles change peoples' lives and therein lies the truth. I have a gift for you. Everyone who stays with us leaves with this. Here, open it."

Sam takes the package, removes the gift wrap, and sees a book entitled, "Seven Secrets for Living Life Abundantly" written by Paul Fisher. She smiles.

"Thank you. I will read it and reread it. Thank you very much for everything. I've never spent a more interesting three days in my life. Maybe they're the most important three days of my life. Could I ask a small favor?"

Paul speaks, "Sure, what can we do for you?"

"May I make one more visit to your secret garden and visit the flower garden? No camera I promise."

"Yes." Paul is moved to ask, "Would you like to do that by yourself?"

"Please."

"Paul," Marilyn says. "Your parents called and they're coming over to visit this weekend."

Sam smiles.

Chapter 29

Aim at heaven and you will get earth thrown in.
Aim at earth and you will get neither.
—C. S. Lewis
20ᵗʰ century Irish author, Scholar of medieval literature,
Essayist and Christian apologist.
Wrote the children fantasy series,
The Chronicles of Narnia.

Sam finds her way to the gate hidden by the vines, opens it, and quietly walks to the area of the brilliant flowers. This time they are even more brilliant. It's a beauty she has never seen, and she sees it unlike she did before with greater reverence and greater clarity.

As she gazes upon the beauty before her, she ponders what she has been shown and told. As to The Master Teacher, who was he? Was he a creation of Paul's imagination? If so, how does one explain the evidence? Was he once a great teacher on earth who, in the spirit world, was summoned to teach Paul the powerful seven strategies? Was he an angel of God? Was he . . . well, maybe it is just too great a question to attempt to answer. Then Sam thought, just maybe he is someone different to each person who listens to his message. Maybe truth can be delivered in many ways when one is ready to hear it. Maybe that is an important lesson here.

Sam felt compelled to kneel and pray. For nearly an hour, Sam prayed and wept and continued to pray. Upon completion, she rose to feel a peace and a strength she hadn't felt before. She smiled and believed all she had been told was true. She knows she will leave this place with a rebirth of enthusiasm for what life will bring her.

Epilogue

Sam returns to the airport to begin her long journey back to the city. She no longer harbors any fear of whether the story will meet with the approval of her editor, Vince. She is happy with her trip and will accept any consequences with gratitude and a spirit of learning from it. As she walks through the doors of the small airport, her attention is drawn toward a homeless man sitting nearby on the floor with a sign that reads, "Will Work for Food." She approaches the man with a newfound empathy. She reaches in her purse and pulls out a couple of dollar bills and hands them to him.

"Thank you, Ma'am. You are kind," he says.

"You are welcome."

As she walks away, he calls to her. "Hey, you've been out to Paul's."

Sam turns, "Yes. How did you know that?"

"Saw the book you're carryin'. He gives that to all the suckers he gets out there. No offense."

"What do you know of Paul?" Her journalistic instincts take over.

"Quite a lot. Met him a few years ago downtown. Me and a buddy was drinkin' a beer on the sidewalk together, and Paul introduced hisself to us. Gave us all that talk about wantin' to help us. Wantin' to get us jobs at McDonald's. All that bull."

"What happened?"

"I could see through it. He just wanted to put a feather in his cap. Be a big shot. You know the type. We went to his house a couple of times. Gave me that same book."

"Didn't work for you, huh?"

"Nope. Why would I go to work at McDonald's for seven dollars an hour when I make more than that sittin' here? So he can feel better about hisself? Don't think so."

"Did he show you the grounds?" Sam did not want to acquaint him with the secret garden and the special flower garden if he was not familiar. She left Paul's home feeling the reverence and sacred nature of that very special place.

"Yeah, you mean did he show me that secret garden place?" Laughing . . . "The, oh-so-special place where you can't take pictures? I saw it. He let me go out there alone. That was stupid. On my second visit, I snuck in a camera. Heck, I took a picture of it."

"You took a photo of it?"

"Yeah, it's right here." He digs for his wallet, worn and falling apart, filled with worthless outdated coupons and crumpled one dollar bills. From the mess, he pulls a Polaroid photo.

"Here it is." He hands the dirty and smudged photo to Sam.

Sam looks at it carefully. Sure enough, it was the garden. The unique wall covered with vines was the backdrop of his photo. He had to be standing at the exact location where she stood looking at the exact place where this wonderfully unique and beautiful stand of many brilliant flowers stood.

Sam gasped, "There is nothing. The photograph shows nothing but a patch of dirt."

"That's right," he says grinning slyly.

There was not a hint of the beauty she had seen. The photo was empty of the striking and brilliant flowers that exist nowhere in the world but on this patch of dirt. But she knew it was there. It was real. It was all she remembered and not at all like what his image portrayed.

"See," he says, "Much-to-do about nuttin'. You suckers!"

Sam returns the photo to the man and begins to leave when she turns and asks: "What happened to your buddy? Didn't you say there were two of you when you met Paul?"

"Yeah, he did the deal. He's a sucker. He worked at McDonald's doin' all of the dirty work for a minimum wage. Don't know what he's doin' now. Heard he mighta qualified for that land Paul gives away. Don't know for sure. Hey, could you spare maybe another dollar? I could use it."

"Good luck to you." As Sam was about to leave again toward the airport's check-in-counter, she was prompted to turn about one more time to ask one final question of the beggar.

"What was your friend's name?"

He thought for a moment. "Uh, Pedro. Pedro Garcia."

Sam smiled, turned, brushed the dust from her shoes and proceeded into a new and an uncommon success that awaits her.

From the Author

Hope you enjoyed "Life Lessons from Beyond" and that you found it worthy of your time. Your experience in reading "Life Lessons from Beyond" is important to me. Please email me with any thoughts, comments, or questions. Thanks for taking your time and responding to me. And best wishes for your life of uncommon success!

dave@lifelessonsfrombeyond.com

End Notes

1   Solomon 2:15 New Living Translation, 2007. "Catch all of the foxes, those little foxes, before they ruin the vineyard of love, for the grapevines are blossoming!" Translation: It is the constant repeating of the small sins we commit that destroy our lives (the fruit of life).

2   Study referencing induced out-of-body experience with electrodes planted in brain. November, 2007, Belgian study reported in New England Journal of Medicine including Dirk De Ridder, MD, PhD, University Hospital Antwerp.

3   Andrew Carnegie, 1835-1919, was considered a 'Captain of Industry.' He earned his fortune in the steel industry and was the second wealthiest man in the world at the time.

4   Story of Andre Carnegie earning first $35 check. Wikipedia.org

5   Biblical principle . . . Believe that the thing you ask for that you already have, and you will have. Mark 11:24 says, "Therefore I say unto you, what things so ever ye desire, when ye pray, believe that ye receive them, and ye shall have them."

6   Leo Corydon Hoyt, 1909-1981, was a renowned American gun engraver from the 1950s through the 1970s and was father of the author.

7   Story of engraver L. C. Hoyt. Conversation with his son, David Hoyt, author, explaining that you must first see in your mind's eye what it is that you want to have happen before you can make it happen.

8   Jim Carrey story. Wikipedia.org

9   Proverbs 18:21 says, "Death and Life are in the power of the tongue; and they that love it shall eat the fruit thereof."

10   Henry Ford, 1863-1947, was an American industrialist and founder of Ford Motor Company. He created the assembly line technique of mass production.

11   Concept . . . "Your life events cannot rise above the words you speak. In fact, you are the sum total of what you have said about yourself, your life, and your circumstances." Fred Price, Power of Positive Confession, DVD series from "Ever Increasing Faith."

12   Dr. Martin Seligman is a noted psychologist, Professor of Psychology, and an accomplished author and research psychologist.

13   "Learned Optimism" by Martin Seligman, PhD

14   Napoleon Hill, 1883-1970, was an American author and was one of the pioneers in writing books on how to attain personal success, an industry now known as "self-help." His book, "Think and Grow Rich" is one of the best-selling books of all time. He was an advisor to President Franklin D. Roosevelt from 1933-1936.

15   Conversation with Krista Evans in regard to her testimony as to how she feels God influences our lives as she feels He has hers.

16   Thomas Jefferson, 1743-1826, was a founding father of the United States, third President, and principal author of The Declaration of Independence.

17   In the New Testament, James 2:20 says "Faith without works is dead."

18   Toastmasters International is a nonprofit international, educational organization that operates clubs for the purpose of helping members improve their communication, public speaking and leadership skills. For additional information, visit its web site at www.toastmasters.org.

19   Mohammad or Muhammad, 570-632, was the founder of Islam and believed to be a Prophet of God. Many of his sayings were passed down orally and

therefore, subject to debate. Although this is one of those such sayings, his wisdom and spoken words about the subject of the struggles of man would justify attributing this quote to him.

20   St. Augustine lived from <u>354-430</u>. St. Augustine is considered an important figure in the development of western Christianity. He is celebrated on his birthday August 28.

21   Charles Montesquieu, <u>1689-1755</u>, was a French philosopher, social commentator, and political thinker.

22   Mohandas Karamchand Gandhi, <u>1869-1948</u>, was the political and ideological leader of India. He believed that non-violent civil disobedience can profoundly change history and free peoples from the tyranny of oppressive governments and his acts started a movement across the globe.

23   William James, <u>1842-1910</u>, was an American pioneer of modern psychology and is considered the Father of Psychology. His godfather was Ralph Waldo Emerson. He wrote The Principles of Psychology, volumes I and II totaling more than 1200 pages.

24   Matthew 10:14 says, "And whosoever shall not receive you, nor hear your words, when ye depart out of that house or city, shake off the dust of your feet."

25   Mihaly Csikszentmihalyi is a Hungarian psychology professor at Claremont Graduate University. He emigrated here from Hungary at age 22 and his work in the study of happiness and creativity is notable. Martin Seligman, the noted psychologist who is also the former president of the American Psychological Association said Mihaly Csikszentmihalyi is the world's leading authority on 'Positive Psychology.'

26   The law of reaping what you sow is spoken many times in the Bible including Mark 4:14-20, Galatians 6:7-9, Matthew 13: 24-25, and Corinthians 9:9-12.

27   2 Corinthians 9:6-7 says: "But this I say: He who sows sparingly will also reap sparingly, and he who sows bountifully will also reap bountifully. So let

each one give as he purposes in his heart, not grudgingly or of necessity; for God loves a cheerful giver."

28   Og Mandino, <u>1923-1996</u> was an American author who wrote 19 inspirational books. His books have sold more than 50 million copies.

29   Alma Hoyt, <u>1914-1987</u>. Story of Alma and genealogy work. Alma Hoyt was mother of David Hoyt and member of the Church of Jesus Christ of Latter-Day-Saints and was a tireless worker for the Church copying records of hundreds of thousands of tombstones and providing those records to state libraries to preserve their records for generations to come.

30   Matthew 19:24 says, "It is easier for a camel to go through the eye of a needle, than for a rich man to enter into the kingdom of God." Rich man here is used in a derogatory manner and was meant as a person who worships money, shares it with no one, and is not using his money to be a blessing to anyone. The concept has been carried over in terms like "filthy rich."

31   There are many scriptures throughout the Bible as to the promises of abundant living for those who serve Him. Among them are . . . Matthew 6:31-33, Hebrews11: 6, John 5:14-15, Proverbs 3:9-10, Proverbs 10:24, Proverbs 10:27, Proverbs 11:25, Ecclesiastes 5:19, Isaiah 58:10-11, Leviticus 26:3-5, 2 Chronicles 31:21. Just look at the simple way that Psalm 23:1 speaks . . . "The Lord is my Shepherd; I shall not want."

32   Cicero was a Roman philosopher. He lived from 106 BC to 43 BC and was a statesman, lawyer, and philosopher. He was a person with power in his words. He was considered one of the great orators during his time.

33   www.daratores.com.

34   Ray Kroc, <u>1902-1984</u>, was an American entrepreneur and is credited with founding McDonald's Corporation and today's fast-food industry. He was one of the wealthiest men of his era who Time Magazine called one of the 100 most important people of the 20th Century.